...uld they be a badger's territorial marks?

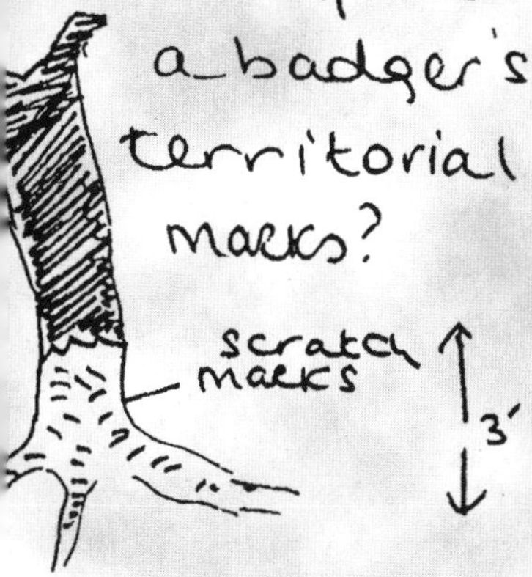

scratch marks ↑ 3' ↓

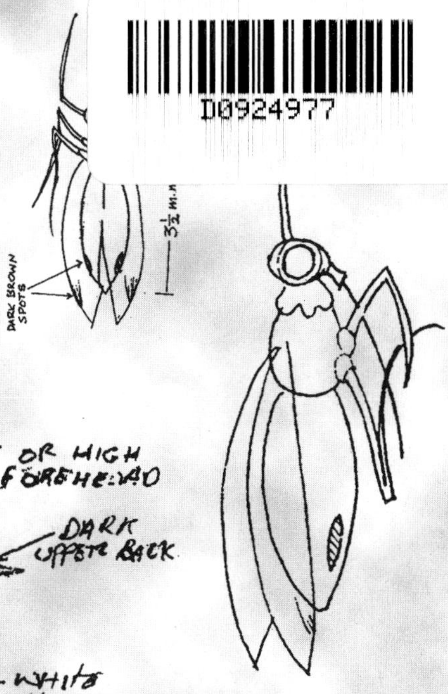

DARK BROWN SPOTS

3½ in.

CREST OR HIGH FOREHEAD

DARK UPPER BACK

WHITE PLUMAGE

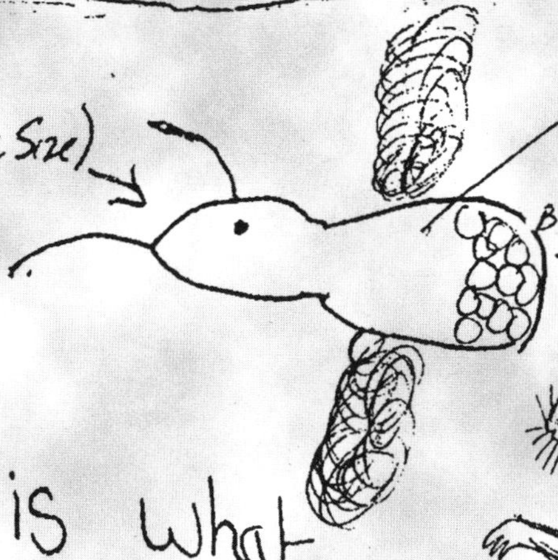

MOUSE BROWN PLUMAGE?

(ACTUAL SIZE) →

BLACK AND WHITE

...s is what ...e or she looks like (Sort of) →

Can you tell me why he has no tail? this way or did he have an accident

The editors gratefully acknowledge the contribution of the correspondents to *Eye on Nature* and dedicate this book to them.

A Wildlife
Narrative

Eye on Nature

MICHAEL & ETHNA VINEY

More than twenty years ago Michael and Ethna Viney left their media jobs in the city to live a more or less self-sufficient life on the west coast. An important part of that life was a closer relationship with nature and study of natural history. They live on a hillside above the ocean and write or make film documentaries about the countryside of Ireland.

A Wildlife Narrative

Eye on Nature

Michael and Ethna Viney
and readers of The Irish Times

IRISH TIMES BOOKS

First Published 1999 by The Irish Times Limited
10 - 16 D'Olier Street Dublin, 2 Ireland.

© Michael and Ethna Viney
© Illustrations Michael Viney

Distribution: Irish Times General Services
Telephone (01) 6792022 Ext. 271
Fax (01) 6718446
email itbooks@irish-times.ie

10 9 8 7 6 5 4 3 2 1

ISBN 0 907011 27 6

Cover design: Terry Foley
Book design: Brenda McNiff
Typeset in Adobe Garamond and printed in Dublin Ireland
by Mahons Printing Works Ltd.

CONTENTS

ILLUSTRATIONS

PREFACE

For all sorts of historical reasons, Ireland came rather late to an 'interest in nature'. Without an industrial revolution to herd people into cities and set the countryside apart, nature was the ordinary, utilitarian world outside the door. Outside of the field clubs of Belfast and Dublin, there was none of the passion for natural history which, in Victorian Britain, filled train excursions to hunt for ferns, butterflies or sea-shells. The classic English books on nature, such as *Tarka the Otter*, had no counterparts in Ireland. This sort of romantic sensibility, and the interests that go with it, belonged in Ireland mostly to an Anglo-Irish minority.

The enormous change of recent decades is part of Ireland's general cultural advance. It has owed a great deal to wildlife films on television and to the ecological concern now sweeping the western world. It has also been fostered by the enthusiasm of school-teachers, by field trips and school wildlife gardens. Bird-tables are commonplace, not only in the middle-class suburbs but in small country towns and among the farms beyond. Groups such as Irish Birdwatch and the Irish Wildlife Trust have a countrywide, mainstream membership.

It was in this context that *Eye on Nature* began in *The Irish Times*, in 1988 as a tentative forum for readers' observations and questions. It quickly moved from the letters about first cuckoos and giant puffballs to explore an extraordinarily wide range of species and wildlife behaviour. Thousands of readers have written letters: not all of them, of course, published. Some of them have become regular contributors, but every week has brought new names and perspectives. 'Is this unusual?' has become a ritual final line, often from people genuinely unsure whether something is worth remarking.

Often it has been unusual, even, at first sight, bizarre: stoats making fish dizzy in rock pools, field mice digging out winkles, ravens snatching up golf balls. Few events of this sort are unprecedented, but they become doubly interesting when they help us see an animal, bird or insect with fresh understanding. Some observations are fascinating because of what they suggest about complex ecosystems: for example, wasps and red admirals crowding to feed at the 'honeydew' produced by aphids on a tree. Insights of this sort, closely observed, can make real contributions to natural science as well as an intriguing story. Records of rarities are valuable, too, if by no means a prime concern. The summer of 1997 brought, for example, two fresh sightings of cornflowers, the beautiful 'weeds' of grain crops that have been rendered all but extinct by modern farming methods.

A surprising interest in insects has burgeoned among readers in the last few years, even in creatures once quite unpopular, to say the least. Spiders, moths, beetles of all sorts, worms and larvae are regular candidates for comment or query. This is part of a conscious awakening to parallel lives around us, a part of placing ourselves *within* nature, as fellow species, rather than insulating ourselves, all unseeing.

There are enviable encounters in this book: 'sprinting' with dolphins off Mayo, for example, or stroking the head of a young whale in a cove in west Cork. Both these correspondents had obviously been deeply moved and excited. But there are also the quiet rewards of treating garden birds and insects as neighbours, of attending day by the day the rhythms and crucial events of their lives. It is in the revelation of the ordinary that *Eye on Nature* has given its greatest value and satisfaction.

Both of us have been involved in the column from an early stage, but Ethna has brought her own particular talent for tracking down a difficult identification or solution to a puzzle. The book we have put together is the testimony of the converted. It reflects the extraordinary variety of the readers' observations, and the fascination of the detail as the descriptive drawings on the end papers will testify. We trust it will encourage another decade of observations for *Eye on Nature*.

Michael and Ethna Viney, Thallabawn, Co Mayo.

ONE

A COMMOTION OF CROWS

 A couple who live on one of those long drumlin peninsulas that jut out into Clew Bay, looking through a telescope, saw three otters fishing in the sea below them. Parents and a cub, they thought. 'When they reached the rocks and climbed out we could see that one of the parents had caught an eel. They presented this to junior and left him ashore to eat it. While he crunched away, however, two hooded crows landed beside him with apparent designs on the eel. One of them pecked the otter on the tip of the tail and then on the rump. He jumped each time he was pecked but didn't stop eating. The parents were about fifty metres offshore and we could hear them calling him. When all the eel had gone he joined them in the sea and the crows flew off in disgust.'[1]

Michael had a similar experience on Thallabawn Strand. One morning, quite unconcealed, he watched as a young otter emerged from the foam about thirty metres ahead, with a small fish in its mouth. It ran, in the usual humped, ungainly way across the strand and up into the dunes, there to eat its fish in a hollow among the marram grass. Out of nowhere a raven appeared and hung above the otter, claws dangling, and uttering a threatening *Caa! Caa! Caa!* Then it touched down nearby, wings lifted, neck outstretched. This was too much, the otter fled back to the sea, while the raven lifted and wheeled away to more usual scavengings on carrion along the shore.

Piracy is something we associate with the more aggressive seabirds, such as the skuas and the larger gulls, but plenty of bullying goes on between the crows. The piratical behaviour of grey or hooded crows was reported by another observer who watched one mobbing a rook in the nest-building season. Eventually the rook dropped the stick it was carrying,

1

and the grey crow caught it in mid-air and flew off.[2]

The crow family, the Corvidae, have accounted for more observations over the years than any other. Several readers have blamed the rooks for maliciously ripping up their lawns in early autumn. 'Can you suggest any reason why rooks have stripped bare part of a lawn? Up to twelve at a time, during two weeks in September, they tore up tufts of grass leaving a bare patch about 20ft by 16ft under a eucalyptus tree.'[3] The rooks were, most probably, feeding on leatherjackets. The larvae of the cranefly or daddy-long-legs which, in turn, feed on the roots or grasses. We see the same behaviour among the choughs, which, with bright red bills, stab after grubs in the lawn-like turf behind the dunes.

Choughs and ravens are the most domestically private of the crow family, nesting remotely on mountains and sea cliffs. As ravens feed mainly on carrion, they rarely draw much human opprobrium. But one reader had a complaint against them. 'On the last two occasions that I played golf at Ballyliffen near Carndonagh in Co Donegal, a raven flew down and took my ball. The golf links in question are in wild dune land and far removed from habitation. On the first occasion it was a white ball, on the second it was yellow. Why would the raven take the balls and where would it eventually deposit them?'[4] Our guess was that the raven thought the golf balls were eggs, and would discard them wherever it alighted to eat them. This was not an isolated incident: a reader in Schull, on the Cork coast, complained of 'crows', unspecified, 'lifting balls, both white and coloured, from the fairways of our golf course during play. They carry some into the gorse on the perimeter of the course, while considerable numbers have been found on the strand on the opposite side of the harbour.'[5]

Choughs made the day for an eleven-year-old visitor to the Dingle peninsula in 1994. 'I went on an expedition with my family in the Kerry mountains near Dingle. It was an exhausting climb but the view at the other side was astounding. It looked like nobody had seen it before, not a person or house in sight. We saw a flock of about fifty jet black birds swirling and swooping and screeching eerily. They had deep red legs and beaks and my father said they were choughs and were virtually extinct.'[6] A flock of choughs engaged in aerobatics, their cries ringing off the rocks, can be a marvellous encounter. In Britain and Europe, their habitats have dwindled severely, and the west and south coasts of Ireland have become their last stronghold. Indeed, the Dingle choughs are now believed to be Europe's largest colony.

A constant flow of letters to *Eye on Nature* comes from urban readers upset by the predatory behaviour of magpies, seen as the murderous yobbos of the bird world: 'I saw a magpie chasing two small songbirds into long grass. After a few seconds of commotion I'm sure the magpie flew off with a bird in its beak. The remaining songbird flew to a neighbouring Scots pine where it sang in a most distressed way for a long time.'[7] Several painstaking studies have shown that magpie numbers have no long-term effect on the wider songbird populations, but raids on fledglings are brutally dramatic and noisy and certainly leave individual gardens, and houses, in a state of shock. The quick swoop of the sparrowhawk, to snatch up a fledgling and whisk it quickly out of sight, is not resented nearly so much when glimpsed through the kitchen window. At least half of all songbirds hatched each year die for one reason or another, but enough survive to maintain numbers. Cats, on the other hand, do more damage because they kill adult birds in winter and so deplete the breeding stock.

Dublin has the largest magpie population of all European cities, so there are regular reports from there of large flocks, particularly in the suburbs. Some of these gatherings are to feed, some to gang up on a predator, others are mysterious assemblies which invite the description 'ceremonial'.

Magpies attack all kinds of competing predators from cats to sparrowhawks. One reader watched a skirmish with a stoat; another watched the bird mob a fox and drive it away. A regular antagonist is the sparrowhawk which is a competitor in nest robbing, and given a chance, will prey on magpie nestlings. One spring, a Co Clare observer heard the screeching of a bird in a nearby field. 'One by one, attacking magpies congregated on the terrified prey with their aggressive tommy-gun-like noise. On previous occasions I have reluctantly left nature to take its course, but this time I threw a stone into the nearby bushes and frightened the magpies away. I was amazed to see a big, brown bird, which I took to be a sparrowhawk, seemingly stunned, stand still for a minute then fly away.'[8] The 'tommy-gun-like' call is always used when magpies are mobbing raptors. It calls in reinforcements of neighbouring magpies, and serves to frighten the sparrowhawk.

Cats and magpies square up to each other frequently in their shared territory of the garden. One reader watched two magpies swooping into a tree and squawking noisily. 'A notorious local tom-cat jumped down from the tree and sat on the grass watching a blackbird feeding nearby. The magpies swooped down on the cat and, when he didn't move, one of them flew at the blackbird chasing it away. Was the magpie saving the blackbird's life?'[9] More likely, it would have made breakfast of the blackbird, if it hadn't flown away.

Another reader had a very different cat story: 'Two magpies that have, over the past three years become pets, got used to eating with our three cats. When we moved house about one mile away, the two magpies showed up and have been with us ever since. Have you ever heard of magpies adopting people and cats?'[10]

The ceremonial gatherings of magpies, sometimes thought to be a mating ritual or 'magpie marriage', are usually started by members of the non-breeding flock trying to establish a territory in 'occupied land'. The gatherings are always started by one or two of the non-breeders and the rest gather to evict them or are attracted by the excitement. This is borne out by two correspondents: 'What is known of the "crows' court", a tribunal in which birds get together to execute one of their members? I came across a scene in Wexford where a magpie was killed by other magpies.'[11]

The second correspondent had a kind heart: 'One for sorrow, indeed. I have a magpie seeking refuge in my half-roofed garage, and a very sorry sight he makes. I reckon he has committed some severe magpie sin for he is visited daily by two other magpies who attack him in such a way that they are definitely trying to kill him. What amazes me is that they remember each day to come and have a go at him. The dog also sleeps in the garage and that is what saves him, because the dog sometimes takes exception to the attackers. He has no tail feathers and I am feeding him. I am hoping that the feathers will grow back and that once the breeding season is over he will be forgiven and accepted back into the fold.'[12]

To see magpies in the role of peace-makers is an anthropomorphic misapprehension. 'Recently on the Castle golf-course I noticed a group of five or six crows. Suddenly, a really vicious fight broke out between two of them. A magpie came on the scene, broke up the fight and all the crows scattered. The magpie then calmly flew back into the conifer whence he had come. Why did the magpie intervene?'[13] This was, almost certainly, a territorial stand rather than an exercise in law and order. The magpie was chasing rowdy interlopers out of its territory; it could also have had food buried nearby.

The "crows' court" is a phenomenon on which several readers remarked. 'My husband shot a grey crow which was squawking from high up on a large oak tree growing outside the door. Shortly after two more landed, and he shot one of those also. The other vanished. About half an hour later I went out to dispose of the bodies and the oak tree was occupied by a noisy gathering of rooks and magpies, although usually there would only be one or two of those at a time. Were they protesting, gossiping, rejoicing or what?'[14] Most of the crow family, particularly rooks, magpies and jackdaws, are drawn to sources of drama. Their noisiness may be an expression of alarm at the presence of an unsuspected predator. They were also, perhaps, 'scolding' the man with the gun, and the wife who went out to clean up was the recipient.

People find the flocking and roosting of rooks a fascinating part of local life. 'From dawn each morning hundreds of rooks begin their daily exodus from their roosting place, passing directly over my house and calling raucously. Looking up, the sky seems full of them, waves of birds reminiscent of old films of "thousand-bomber flights". The "fly-over" takes an average of fifteen minutes, the height they fly at depending on the weather, the finer, the higher. Recently, with a friend, I watched the rooks mobbing what I think was a sparrowhawk, but we lost sight of this aerial battle after a few minutes.'[15] Communal roosting, nesting and foraging is obviously advantageous to rooks, but, to be anthropomorphic ourselves, they may also like the company.

Crows will often flock over a source of food, which seems to be the case in the following observation: 'We have witnessed great numbers of jackdaws on occasion flying in an hysterical manner, while still remaining in the same general area. Recently we saw the more unusual sight of maybe one hundred grey crows behaving likewise.'[16] Perhaps there was rubbish dumped there. In the leaner countryside, the filling of a food trough or the death of a sheep will often draw the local crows.

Jackdaws can test the patience and tolerance of householders in the nesting season, when they try, with great determination, to take up residence in chimneys. Their technique is classic. They patiently drop twigs into the chimney until one and then more become stuck; then they build the nest on that foundation. But one pair of jackdaws in Co Sligo, using the same tireless method, built a bizarre structure. 'Jackdaws have built a nest thirteen feet high in our outhouse. They started by dropping in twigs and other material through an opening in a ventilation window. When we closed the window they came in by another window, completed the structure and raised a brood.'[17] An accompanying photograph showed this astonishing edifice: a case of 'I've started, so I'll finish . . .'

All crows are clever and learn quickly from each other. Rooks, ravens and grey crows crack shellfish by dropping them from a height on to rocks. From Antrim: 'I observed a crow alighting on a stony part of the beach, grasp something with its beak, take off and drop the object from a height of about fifty feet. It was using the stones to break the shells of dog whelks. I later saw three crows enjoy such a feast, one had even managed to prize a limpet from its rock. Gulls have learned how much more efficient a nearby concrete promenade is for smashing shells.'[18]

On a cold May evening, another observer saw a pair of crows near a chimney, each in turn hopping on the rim of the chimney pot and spreading the underside of its wings over the smoke. The birds changed position every thirty seconds, and continued with this manoeuvre for more than ten minutes.[19] They might have been warming themselves, but it is also probable that they were using the smoke to rid themselves of parasites.

One of the first letters to *Eye on Nature* ten years ago was from a bird-watcher who heard a rook mimicking another bird. 'Back in January, while digging in the garden, I heard a rook calling hoarsely from an ash tree. Between calls it practised melodiously to itself a distinct cuckoo call. This was done in a confiding manner, rather in the same way that a starling may mimic a curlew; it sounds the same but doesn't carry. I have been a bird-watcher for almost thirty years and never knew a rook could sound so sweet.'[20] Although rooks are not noted for mimicry, we have heard some strangely fowl-like sounds from one rook who used to steal food from our hens!

From the letters to *Eye on Nature* it would seem that jays are the least-observed member of the crow family; correspondents always express surprise. A pair was seen in the Phoenix Park in 1990, and a couple of years later, others in Sandymount and in Ballydehob, Co Cork. Jays are, in fact, not quite so rare as these observations suggest. They are birds of woodland and not often seen elsewhere. At various times, the population has declined, but, as forestry expands, jays are now to be found in almost every county. A Maynooth correspondent regretted their absence in his neighbourhood: 'Twenty-five years ago there were breeding pairs of jays in Carton Estate in an oak wood that has since fallen to commerce, but I haven't seen a jay any place in the last fifteen years.'[21]

Several correspondents noticed that starlings often roost with rooks. 'I have a long-established rookery on about a dozen sycamores alongside my home. This year I counted about thirty-five nests. In August an apparently ever-increasing flock of starlings started roosting there too, and there appears to be no ill-will between the two sets of birds. Will the starlings roost there for the winter?'[22] Large numbers of starlings come in late summer and autumn to our local rookery when they are flocking before the winter, roosting amicably in the conifers beside the rooks' sycamores. Later on they disappear and probably disperse to good feeding areas. Whether starlings remain in a particular roost depends on the rewards at the local feeding sites.

The remarkable pre-roosting flights of starlings occupied the interest of many readers, especially in winter when Ireland's birds are joined by great numbers from north-west Europe. The largest flocks are in the midlands. 'While travelling from Loughrea to Ballinasloe at about 5.30pm, we saw a huge, shimmering, black cloud which constantly changed shape. We were amazed when we got closer to find that it was an enormous flock of starlings. There seemed to be millions of them and they were very noisy.'[23] Another observer had a similar experience at Mullingar: 'What I thought at first was a black twine of smoke or rain cloud, turned out to be what looked like thousands of birds flying in formation. Over the next hour thousands more joined in this incredibly structured bird dance. Two things stood out: the enormous number of birds and the patterned nature of their flight.'[24]

It is really a spectacular sight as these enormous flocks turn, swirl and swoop in perfect synchronisation, like silk scarves caught in a whirlwind, in a last display before they retire to a communal roost. Earlier there would have been a pre-roost assembly in the fields, bringing together large flocks which had foraged separately during the day, perhaps as far as 20km distant. Winter roosts of up to 100,000 birds occur in several counties, and Dublin attracts huge roosts in the city centre, with its warm air and liberal food supply. In Britain, a large winter roost may number up to one million birds.

The aerial displays of all birds hold endless fascination for people who make time to stop and stare. 'I noticed a group of doves flying in a circular pattern. Every now and again one of them tumbled down, spinning as it did so. After a fall of about five metres it would recover and with great effort rejoin the group. Mostly the doves would fall singly, sometimes in pairs. A mating display? But why in a group of nine?'[25] It was indeed a mating display. The bird rises steeply with strong but not rapid wing beats, and then, stiffening its wings, falls and rises again. At the end of this display it makes a clap with a strong downbeat of the wings. This display in a group was unusual, but it may have been a flock from a pigeon loft.

The term 'pigeon' and 'dove' are interchangeable, particularly in local usage. City pigeons are the feral descendants of domesticated pigeons which have returned to the wild, and their common ancestor is the rock dove. Homing or racing pigeons are also descended from the rock dove. Ireland and western Scotland are the only places where true communities of rock doves can now be found; elsewhere they have interbred widely with feral birds. 'Among the pigeons at the back of Trinity College there is a brown one just like a bantam. All the others are nearly black or slate-coloured or speckled light brown. Are Dublin pigeons descended from those that were kept for food?'[26] More than likely they are, but others may have come in from the country to the warmth and food of the city. Hand-rearing and selection have played genetic havoc with their original colour of blue-grey plumage and glossy, green and lilac neck.

'While climbing trees near our home my two young sons discovered some pigeons' nests. They are what we call "tame" pigeons. Two of the nests have each got two eggs and a bird sitting on them, and a third has two chicks just hatched out. Is this unusual for mid-September?'[27] All pigeons and doves have two or three broods in the year, sometimes more if the weather is fine; and the number of eggs is always two.

TWO

THRUSH ON A MERRY-GO-ROUND

 In the quiet days between Christmas and the New Year, a Kilkenny correspondent went for five walks along the banks of the River Nore, and later wrote of the exhilaration and joy of her discoveries. 'Each day I saw something new and exciting. I saw my first goldcrest close-up in the branches of a bare tree, and a redwing on its own. I disturbed a heron feeding at the water's edge, and saw up to twenty siskins picking over a bushy tree that had withered seed pods. On the same day, about fifty yards further on, were a similar number of long-tailed tits on another bush; they let me approach quite close. I sat on a log and watched a tree creeper work the trunk of a big old tree; and a strange, distant sound turned out to be five swans flying in V-formation low over the water, honking as they flew past. A robin came out one day and accompanied me for almost two miles of the walk. Or was it several robins, each in his own territory? There were pigeons in the tall trees, blackbirds flitting from the lower branches, and I put up a cock pheasant whose squawk put the heart across me. Since then, on the same walk, I have been rewarded with sand martins, grey wagtails and two beautiful kingfishers.'[1]

The pleasure which resident birds provide at bird tables, in hedgerows and woodland or nesting in incongruous places, has been echoed by many readers.

The very first letter to *Eye on Nature* was from a Tipperary woman who became a regular correspondent. She had a song thrush that nested year after year in the strangest situation. 'For the fourth year, a thrush has built her nest in the axle of our electric horse exerciser, a merry-go-round for half-a-dozen horses, of the sort that many stud farms have. She is happily nursing four eggs in the nest, which is only about four-and-a-half feet off the ground; and besides the usual moss and grass she has used bits of cotton wool and bandaging found around the stables. Last year she reared two clutches, sitting quite contentedly on the merry-go-round. If she happens to be out feeding when it is switched on, she sits on the perimeter wall screeching until someone stops the mechanism. Then she flies in happily and away it goes again.'[2]

The song thrush can also surprise its human neighbours by choosing to sing at night. A mystery surrounds one nocturnal singer. 'On March 25th I heard a song thrush singing in the garden at 1 am. It was still singing merrily when I went to bed at 1.45 am. Maybe it mistook the lights for the dawn, but if so why did it only make a mistake on that morning?' A year later: 'For the record, the same thrush presumably gave a repeat performance on the same tree, at the same time and date this year. Later that day he was back on the tree for another singing session.'[3]

Thrushes are also noted for their mimicry; they have been recorded copying the calls of many birds, including blackbird, lapwing, whimbrel and mallard. A reader near the Moy River discovered this much to his surprise. 'My neighbour across the way dropped over for a few minutes. Says I, after the usual chit-chat, weather, fishing, etc, "Ye have got ducks". "No" he says, "what you heard was a bird that looks a lot like a thrush but makes these duck noises - *quack-quack*." I heard it again yesterday and stood for a good while listening to it.'[4]

Blackbirds, the more excitable cousins of the song thrush, occasionally sing at night, sometimes to most moving effect: 'Very late one cold, dark winter's night, I heard a blackbird singing. I opened my front door, turned out all the lights in the house and sat by the fire and listened as he sang his heart out for thirty minutes. He went through every permutation of his incredible repertoire, and when he stopped his song seemed to hang on the still, frosty air. It was pure magic and a memory I shall treasure for the rest of my life.'[5]

Sometimes people are taken aback when they see a contradiction in terms: a white or partially white blackbird. Every year, albino or partially albino birds are reported, usually in suburban gardens, and while few, they are not rare; the condition seems to occur less frequently in other birds. True albinism, total lack of colour in the feathers, irides and soft parts is thought by some experts to be a recessive gene and to be hereditary. They also consider, however, that partially white birds, which usually retain normal colour otherwise, may be suffering from diet deficiency, perhaps too much dependence on the food from bird tables, old age, injury or shock. In partially albino blackbirds, the white area tends to spread as they get older. There have also been reports of albino swallows, sparrows, crows, thrushes and mallards, even an oystercatcher, which kept black primary feathers in its wings, and its bright red bill.

Cats are the enemy, if not always mortal, of blackbirds. 'In early spring my cat brought in a cock blackbird and littered the floor with feathers which were quite large. I finally found the bird on a window ledge minus his tail but otherwise unhurt. He flew across the lawn when I put him out. Is he likely to survive or will the loss of his tail feathers inhibit his flight and leave him open to attack.'[6] It may inhibit his breeding and feeding duties, but blackbirds moult their feathers in late summer anyhow and still manage to survive.

The melodramatic skelter of blackbirds in the currant bushes on human approach is well known to gardeners, but one correspondent was resentful at this poaching. 'The fruit crop brought the tiresome chore of netting it against the ravages of the birds, especially the brazen blackbird. Our hedgerows are laden with blackberries of a wonderful size and flavour. Why do our birds show a calculated disdain for the luscious fruits in their own exclusive habitat?'[7] The garden is as much the territory of the blackbird as of the human owner; and the hedgerows are no less the habitat of humans than of blackbirds. The English ornithologist, Rev P H T Hartley, spent some time observing the wild-fruit preferences of the thrush family. He found that blackberries were not a general food with thrushes. But in western Cornwall in the early mornings, he saw blackbirds, song thrushes and robins feeding regularly on them. Foxes and dogs like them, too.

All birds suffer from parasites such as lice and fleas, and blackbirds and thrushes sometimes have problems with *Ornithomia avicularia*, a parasite bird-fly called the louse fly or bird ked. 'I found a dazed, female blackbird in the garden, and after several efforts to fly she died. As she died, from under her feathers came an insect about the size of a housefly. It was light grey in colour, and seemed to be adapted to a parasitic way of life, with a very tough exterior and unusually strong-looking legs and strange large feet or suckers. It tried to land on me but I frightened it away. Do birds often carry parasites like that, or does this one attack any animal?'[8] This fly also lives on owls and pigeons and is around from June to October, usually on young birds because older ones preen more thoroughly.

Humans, gardeners in particular, probably have a more intimate relationship with the robin than with any other resident bird. 'One of the pleasures of gardening is to have friendly robins hopping around as one works. When moving earth I sometimes have to stop while a robin selects a worm from the wheelbarrow. Recently I lost one of my red-breasted friends. I had just finished earthing up a drill of potatoes and was having a short rest when a sparrowhawk swooped and grasped a robin just five metres away from me. Before I could react he had flown away with his prey.'[9]

Robins are also great opportunists and *Eye on Nature* has had some strange reports about them. 'In my local park I witnessed a robin fishing in some shallow water along the banks of a stream. It was a cold morning and the robin perched on a twig just above the water. It studied the water carefully and then suddenly took flight, skimmed the water with its beak, picked something from the surface and resumed its perch. It battered a medium-sized stickleback against a branch and swallowed the catch head first. This was repeated several times until the robin disappeared into a hedge. I must add that a kingfisher was fishing too, just yards away. Might the robin have been copying it?'[10]

David Lack, the greatest living authority on the robin, mentioned a wide variety of food: caterpillars, all kinds of insects, earthworms, spiders, seeds, berries and small fruits, and of course anything left on the bird table, but he certainly missed sticklebacks!

The cock and the hen robin look alike and can be told apart only by physical examination. Frustrated robin-watching must have been what pushed J P Burkitt, county surveyor of Fermanagh (1900-1940), into trapping all the robins in his garden and putting different patterns of metal rings on their legs, thus launching a technique for which ornithology is eternally grateful. 'A robin which has made his or her home in our garden all winter has recently acquired a mate. Is the newcomer a *sliabh isteach*, a landless young man who marries a young woman with a farm? I have no trouble discerning the gender of all the other small birds that come to our feeder, but the robin baffles me.'[11] Usually it is the cock that holds a territory during the winter, but occasionally a gender-liberated hen can do so too.

Sometimes a lucky garden owner can observe a robin marriage.

'Earlier in spring two robins faced each other on the wall outside my window, where they performed a most beautiful, syncopated dance, bowing slightly to either side. It was like a ballet.'[12] Another reader saw a different aspect of robin courtship: 'Recently I observed a robin feeding a worm to another adult robin, Might this have been one of last year's brood still being favoured, or could it be a mating ritual?'[13] This was an example of courtship feeding, which in robins starts in late March and continues throughout the breeding season.

In the same yard where a thrush built a nest in an electric horse exerciser, a robin built a nest under the bonnet of a car and laid three eggs in it before the travels of the car caused her to abandon the nest. Another robin built a nest in a storage bin in the noisy machine shop of an engineering firm. 'There are four chicks and both parents are busy either feeding them or sitting on the nest. The constant noise and frequent passing by of people doesn't seem to bother them.'[14]

Robins are very territorial and the male, as mentioned above, often holds his territory from one breeding season to the next. 'In late January, the cat next door killed my resident robin. Three days later, five robins flew into my garden, perched for a while and then left. Did they come to avenge the dead or to take up the territory?'[15] They came to prospect the territory; they probably missed the dead robin's song and realised that the coast was clear.

Blue tits often draw attention to themselves by pecking at windows. This is not an avian attempt to communicate with the cave dwellers, sometimes there may be insects on the glass. More likely still, the tit is attacking his reflection in defence of his territory, and this behaviour can begin even in winter if the weather is mild. 'For several weeks,' a correspondent wrote in February, 'a blue tit spent several hours pecking at the glass of my office window. He does this while in flight. I noticed that he is doing the same to windows of adjoining houses. Tits have nested in the down pipes of my house for the past ten years but I have never seen this behaviour before.'[16]

Many different birds attack their reflections in windows, thinking that they are repelling a trespasser on their territory. This seems to be increasing with the spread of double-glazing, which can catch the light and reflections of trees and sky in a mirror-like way. When the problem is serious, cut-outs of hawks hung in the window may deter the kamikaze birds.

'A food source for tits that may have been largely overlooked is nectar,' says Christopher Perrins, author of *British Tits*, who has studied the birds for many years. 'Further studies of the amount of nectar taken by birds in the wild would be useful,' he said. But one *Eye on Nature* correspondent spotted this behaviour away back in 1988. 'Opposite and fairly close to our kitchen windows grows a large bush of flowering currant, *Ribes sanguineum*. Several years ago, and ever since, I noticed that blue tits were moving through it, looking, I thought, for insects. Not so, it was nectar they were after! First they flicked off one of the tiny petals, then drank deeply before moving on to the next nectar-full blossom. This year the storm destroyed all but one of the blossoms, but I saw a blue tit making the most of it.'[17]

Another letter that year added an extra dimension to the blossom theme: 'We have several lovely wild cherries in our garden. In mid-April I observed a blue tit flitting among the branches, with another tit close by. Several times he pulled off a whole blossom and faced the other tit, shaking the blossom to and fro and then dropped it.'[18] This is a courtship ritual that continues long after the original mating display. Blue tit females go through a food begging display to their mates during the laying season when they require extra food for egg formation, and this delightful performance must have been part of that activity.

Every year the restaurateurs to the bird kingdom, the bird-table providers, worry about keeping nuts on the menu during the nesting period. Conventional wisdom holds that nut particles are indigestible by the young nestlings and kill them. This may well be true, and perhaps it is better to be sure than sorry. But the natural food for young blue tits is caterpillars. Egg-laying is timed every year, in response to some as yet unknown factor that also relates to the caterpillar season, so that the nestlings appear at the height of caterpillar abundance. If such a strong correlation exists, the danger of blue tits feeding nuts to their young may not be very real.

Nuts, or rather a nut container, became a different kind of hazard to a great tit in Cork. 'Outside the kitchen window of our suburban flat we have a bird bath on a pedestal, hung with a plastic saucer of crumbs mixed with fat, a seed feeder, a coconut in season and until recently, a net bag of peanuts in their shells. One morning we found an unfortunate great tit with a claw trapped in the mesh of the nut bag, and the leg broken from its struggles. Feeling unable to splint the leg, we let the bird go to take its chances. In the days following it appeared with the injured leg hanging down, and then one morning it came with the leg gone and managing very well without it.'[19] Wire mesh nut-holders are probably safer than net bags.

Several bird-lovers had problems attracting blue tits to nesting boxes; the following letter is typical: 'Two years ago I made a blue tit nesting box and fixed it in a twenty-five year old Scots pine in the garden. Four or five blue tits frequent the garden and take seeds from the feeder, but so far none has used the box although it has long since taken on the colour of the tree.'[20] Perhaps the tits don't fancy the layout of the house, or even the locality. A tit box needs a clear flight path to the entrance hole which should have a diameter of 25-30mm and is best placed near the top; there is no need for a landing perch. They should be at least ten metres apart and the internal area should be roughly 120mm x 160mm x 200mm. The box should not be thickly sheltered or darkened by foliage but protected from cold winds. It should face more or less eastward to avoid direct sun on the nestlings.

Left to themselves, blue tits will nest in the most improbable places. One year we had a pair that squeezed through a tiny hole in a breeze block on the corner of a shed, and reared a family inside. Another blue tit, also a Mayo bird, defied gravity. She built a nest 'inside and at the base of a hollow, steel post, the diameter of which is only 75mm and the depth 1,240mm. There are two things I'd like to know: (i) does the bird know there will be a good summer, because surely there is a risk of drowning if it rains; and (ii) will the fledglings be able to reach the top of the post when they hatch?'[21]

Long-tailed tits, with their plumage of pink, white and black are our favourite acrobats among the tits, like a troupe of Arab tumblers. They nest in woodlands, hedgerows, park lands and generally leafy habitats, and in winter flocks leave their breeding grounds and rove about looking for food. One of the engaging things about them is the way they roost at night: all pressed together in a ball, with their tails sticking out, on a branch at the heart of a hawthorn bush. They often use the same place, night after night for several weeks.

They stay out of towns, as a rule, and are infrequent but welcome visitors to bird tables. One Dublin reader enjoyed a visit from them. 'Our back garden backs on to some fine forest trees. Three nut baskets attract blue tits, coal tits and great tits constantly throughout the year, and greenfinches since October.   On December 17th we had a sudden invasion of eight to twelve long-tailed tits which we had not seen for about a year.   They spent all day at the nuts and flitting about the shrubs and trees.   Next morning they were gone.'[22]

Although all the tits that come to bird tables eat the same food, each species has peculiarities in its feeding habits which relate to the ecological niche which it occupies.   The coal tit, for example, is the only Irish tit that hoards food, and one correspondent spotted this idiosyncrasy: 'I placed a new bird feeder in my garden, the type that allows one nut to be taken out at a time.   A coal tit was the first to discover how to get the nuts out.   It took a nut and flew up into a pine tree.   It immediately returned to the feeder, took another nut and flew to a different branch in the pine.   It repeated this operation at least ten times, each time going to a different branch of the pine.   As the coal tit did not have time to eat the nut between flights, was it storing them to eat later?'[23]

The coal tit hides the nuts among the pine needles, usually towards the top of the tree where it hunts.   It generally stores conifer seeds, but will even store insects for later use.   The marsh tit and the willow tit, both of which are absent from Ireland but common in Britain, also store food. There are occasional sightings of vagrant marsh tits in this country, as recorded in the next paragraph.   When feeding at bird tables alongside bigger tits, the coal tit also finds it useful to store the fragments dropped by its competitors.

Tits at the bird-table give enormous pleasure and some observers are concerned that more aggressive birds will displace them.   'Is there any way I can prevent the greenfinches taking almost all the nuts I put out for tits (great, blue, crested, long-tailed and marsh)?'[24]   One way is to buy or make a tit-bell, filling it with solid fat in which nuts are embedded and hanging it in the garden, where only the most agile birds can use it.

The tiny wren ought, one feels, to appreciate some extra food in winter, but it prefers to hunt for spiders in walls and hedge-bottoms than come to the bird-table for crumbs.   It does, however, share some of the tits' roosting habits and nesting-boxes put up for tits are among its chosen dormitories.   Other sorts of nest will do: 'I have heard of groups of wrens gathering together in a cluster in extremely cold weather to provide warmth.   In recent weeks (January) I have found up to a dozen wrens roosting every night in an abandoned swallow's nest in my shed.'[25]

Wrens like to eat butterflies, particularly the small tortoiseshell. 'Every August and September I have a problem with wrens when they attempt to eliminate systematically the scores of tortoiseshells on my *Sedum spectabile* and *Sedum telephium* which I grow specially for butterflies. Careful examination below the plant reveals scores of butterfly wings, and observation reveals how deadly efficient wrens are in catching the butterfly from behind, removing its wings with its beak and then eating the body.'[26]

Wrens are also expert at finding tortoiseshells that hibernate indoors. Just how expert is testified by another correspondent: '1996 was a great year for butterflies and I never saw more small tortoiseshells coming in to hibernate. Late in December a wren came into the house on several occasions and was let out; but he then brought his mate in and the two of them systematically searched every sash window and curtain in this large house leaving carpets and beds strewn with an unbelievable number of butterfly wings, including one peacock. Having drawn all covers, they then left and have not returned. Our neighbours have also noticed wings, and yesterday I saw the same thing happen in the church.'[27]

There is an Irish bird even smaller than the wren, but one not often seen in gardens. 'My cat caught a tiny bird in late October which unfortunately was dead before I could get it from her. It is yellowish in colour, but the unusual thing is it has a tuft of black, orange and yellow feathers on its head. I have not seen one like it before and only hope my cat has not killed the one specimen in my garden.'[28] It is always easier to describe and identify a dead bird. The goldcrest is our smallest species. It spends most of its time in the tops of conifers where it builds a suspended nest, but it sometimes comes down into garden vegetation in winter. It will then join with loose flocks, often with tits, and the cat may have caught a bird that was passing through.

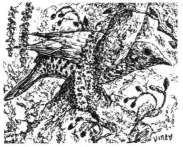

NOTES

THREE

TABLE MANNERS

Among the liveliest visitors to bird-tables are the finches, resident birds which roam the countryside in winter, foraging after the seeds for which their strong bills are designed. Chaffinches and greenfinches feed avidly at seed-hoppers and peanut-bags; goldfinches, too, we find, once thistle-heads are empty. Much of the country has been so sanitised of seeding wildflowers that fewer people get the chance of seeing these colourful, often mixed, flocks of finches foraging in their natural habitats.

Siskins, small and yellow-green, are a new kind of finch to many people, often glimpsed for the first time at a bird-table. They nest in conifer plantations and their numbers have increased with the spread of spruce and pine. At the bird-table they can be aggressive to other birds, yet winter sorties into gardens can sometimes prove fatal. 'Twice recently, observing our well-attended bird-table we were horrified to see a jackdaw take to the air with an adult male siskin in its bill. Have we a rogue jackdaw on our hands, was the siskin simply in the wrong place at the wrong time, or is this common behaviour?'[1] Jackdaws have been known to take bantam chicks and nestlings, so taking a siskin, à la carte, off a bird-table would not be amiss to this opportunistic feeder.

Like the siskins, chaffinches can take time to learn how to take nuts from feeders. A reader watched the process: 'We have put out nuts for birds for several winters. Up to now chaffinches would take nuts that fell on the ground and occasionally try to take them from the holders but fail. However, twice recently I have seen a male chaffinch succeed in taking nuts from the holder.'[2] Another birdwatcher was surprised to see a chaffinch leaping up after flies like a flycatcher,[3] but seed-eating finches turn to insects in the breeding season.

A Co Dublin reader watched the mating display of a pair of chaffinches: 'I saw for the first time a cock chaffinch performing a courtship dance. Crouching down with his wings outstretched and fluttering, he moved in an arc of about 100 degrees for two to two-and-a-half feet as though he were on ball bearings. The hen bird was also crouching and facing the cock. This behaviour lasted for some minutes. Is this a common event?'[4] Common enough, indeed, to ensure survival of the species.

Several correspondents reported seeing chaffinches that were lighter in colour than usual. These were part of the annual winter invasion of Viking female chaffinches. They leave Norway and Sweden, travelling clockwise around the North Sea to avoid long, open sea journeys. The males and some females drop off in Holland, and the remaining females continue on to Ireland. They return home in March and April.

Crossbills are finches that have been coming more and more to the notice of birdwatchers. One correspondent saw two dozen or so on top of conifers in Co Wicklow.[5] They have bred in that county and others, and fresh invasions are making them more plentiful around the country with the spread of conifer plantations.

The brambling, a winter visitor, is another finch newly discovered by readers. They come in October and leave in March, but one stayed on longer in 1992: 'In mid-June a strange bird appeared around our garden in Dublin and his visit lasted two weeks. During that time he perched very high, calling all the time, something like *chi-chi-chi* very quickly, then a gurgle ending with an upward inflection. He resembled a chaffinch but was bigger with a more pointed beak, rosy breast, dark head, white undertail and bars on the wings.'[6] That was, indeed, a brambling which failed to return to Scandinavia, and seemed also to be looking for a mate.

The beautiful scarlet rosefinch, or scarlet grosbeak, a rare vagrant finch, has been making occasional appearances in Donegal, and one visitor to Rossnowlagh is sure he saw one: 'We had several fleeting visits from an exotic finch-type bird. It was a little larger than a linnet or redpoll and had the flight characteristics of a finch. The neck, head and upper breast were vivid crimson or scarlet and the back was a light grey. It lit on clumps of meadowsweet on each visit before flitting away.'[7]

The scarlet grosbeak is a very rare visitor to these islands, but seems to be expanding its European range, and in recent years there have been a few sightings. 'On January 7th, mid-morning, I saw three birds feeding on an old cotoneaster in the garden. Two flew off, but one remained for a minute or two about ten feet from me. It looked like a portly female chaffinch, but it had a beak rather like a bullfinch. It looked exactly like a female scarlet grosbeak as illustrated in *Collins Pocket Guide to British Birds*.'[8]

When the breeding season is over and the new generation of birds are launched on the adventure of life, the family breaks up and most birds take off on a holiday fly-about. The breeding females take time off to moult before they set out, like the others, to find a good source of food and shelter for the winter. 'Around the beginning of November we had a visitor to a third-storey landing window at a roof valley, a bird similar to a wagtail. It is a beautiful bird, yellow undercarriage, grey stripes on back, a very long tail, beak unusually long, very active. He constantly twirls upward and then pecks the glass and seems to be alone. I put out peanuts in a container but he is uninterested.'[9] This was a grey wagtail; the black-and-white one is the pied wagtail; the yellow wagtail is lighter in colour and has yellow underparts and chin; it does not breed in Ireland. The grey wagtail is an insectivore, which is why it scorned the peanuts, and it was catching insects on the wing on its upward twirls. In the breeding season it nests along fast-flowing, stony rivers and streams, but in autumn and winter wagtails leave the breeding grounds and migrate to farms, the roofs of buildings and other urban niches where insect life is found.

Another correspondent had a sad tale about a grey wagtail. 'In autumn a grey wagtail flew into our storeroom and died trying to get out. Ever since, its mate has never gone away. For some weeks it fluttered frantically up and down outside the windows of the room. Three months later it is far less frenzied, but it still leaves the area for only a minute or two at a time. Luckily there is food and water nearby and it seems to feed all right. Short of kidnapping a mate is there anything we can do to relieve the poor bird's distress?'[10] We should always be cautious about assuming that two birds make a pair, at least outside the breeding season, and especially where a supply of food is involved. The second bird's frantic fluttering at the window may be foraging insects on it or trying to get at some on the inside. Grey wagtails are monogamous, but generally stay together only for the breeding season.

A strange tale of a pied wagtail came from a reader in Tipperary. 'If you want a close encounter of the feathered kind go to Coleman's Cross, a couple of miles west of Fethard, where a very curious pied wagtail is waiting on the verge or on a shed. He will hop on to your wing mirror as you pass, then drop back a few feet and fly alongside to see his reflection, perch again and fly to the other mirror if you try opening the window. This performance continues for about half-a-mile until, obviously at the end of his territory he drops off and returns to base. Or you can be kind, as I am, turn the car around and give him a lift home, where he waits for what he thinks is the next invader intruding on his patch. He is a great tourist attraction.'[11]

Pied wagtails seem to be wing-mirror enthusiasts because another one 'fell in love with the mysterious bird in the side mirrors of our car. And some years ago, when a lot of cars had reflective hubcaps, a friend from Dungarvan told me of a veritable dawn chorus of "pings" set up by pied wagtails all over the town attacking what appeared to be rivals in the wheels.'[12]

The private lives of birds can make some observers feel like voyeurs. 'On looking out our kitchen window I spotted movement in the top branches of a tree. It was two sparrows mating. During the short time I watched, they mated seven times in all. Is this normal, or do we have over-sexed sparrows in our back garden?'[13] The sparrows' behaviour was not exceptional. Most birds copulate several times at a session and it is most frequent in the day or two before egg-laying.

Spying on house sparrows is easy because they often nest in roofs. 'When they heard the kitchen window opening, the sparrows which nest in our roof came to the sill for bread crumbs. They craned their necks to look in at us and we came to recognise individual birds.'[14] Another correspondent told of a pair of sparrows that succeeded, after trying for two years, in taking over a house martin's nest, and rearing a brood while the neighbouring house martins swooped and swirled around them, attending their own nests.[15] House sparrows prefer a dry environment, or so it would seem from the way they avoid the wetter halves both of Ireland and Britain.

Distribution maps have stories to tell, often about loss of habitat or changes in food supply. The beautiful yellowhammer, or yellow bunting, has all but vanished from western counties since cultivation of grain crops ceased there, but is still to be found around the cereal farms in the south-east of the country. A large flock arrived on a Wicklow farm one February and stayed for a couple of weeks, but moved on.[16] They typically travel in flocks in winter, moving from farm to farm, feeding mainly on cereal grains and the large seeds of grass and weeds.

Reed buntings, on the other hand, have been doing rather well in Ireland and are found almost everywhere in suitable habitats. The same correspondent who saw the scarlet rosefinch at Rossnowlagh also encountered a reed bunting. 'A male reed bunting lit on the path a few feet behind me and commenced a ritual. The tail feathers were fully extended in a fan shape and it crouched low on the ground, moving a few feet in different directions. Once he had my attention he continued along the path in the same stance, and after thirty or forty feet flew back to where he had first appeared. Could he have been trying to lure me from a nest?'[17] Richard Ussher, in his classic *Birds of Ireland* (1900), recounts this behaviour of reed buntings as follows: 'Birds that have young, especially males, will spread themselves on the ground, like pen-wipers, to divert attention.'

The jewelled flash of a kingfisher always delights observers. *Eye on Nature* readers found them at a tiny inlet near Baltimore, Co Cork, on the Boyne, on tributaries of the Dodder and even, surprisingly, on the Liffey in central Dublin. 'One day in November I was looking over the Capel Street bridge when I saw a brilliant blue streak flashing over the surface of the water. It was a handsome kingfisher and it perched on a block of stone jutting out from the wall about two feet above the surface of the river.'[18]

Readers are slowly coming to know another, much smaller, river bird, far less dashing, but rewarding in a different way. 'During my daily walk on a river bank I have on many occasions seen a bird, bigger than a wagtail but smaller than a thrush. Its plumage is jet-black and it has a snowy white throat and breast. I have not seen it swimming but it ducks into the water and splashes about.'[19] The name this reader wanted was the dipper, and one day she may get a clear view as it walks on the river bed, under the water, seeking its insect food.

The dawn chorus of resident, nesting birds, their mating and territorial warblings, have given pleasure to many, but one letter wanted to know how they did it. 'How do birds produce their songs, the actual sound? It seems to be by a different method to that of human song or instrument. I am very deaf and use a fairly efficient hearing aid, yet without it I can hear bird song perfectly. With the hearing aid I could practically have the bird sitting on my shoulder, while instrumental sound and singing are distorted horribly. The other question is how do birds make their great volume of sound with no evidence of breathing and such tiny lungs?"[20]

Presumably bird song is on a wavelength which the correspondent picks up more easily than human song on his hearing aid. Birds do, indeed, produce sound in a different way. They make it with membranes in the syrinx, an organ found in no other animals, and located where the windpipe forks into the lungs. The sound then travels through the windpipe and into the larynx where it is amplified.

A bird's lungs are, indeed, tiny, but it has extra air sacs distributed all over its body. When a bird inhales, most of the air goes into these, and this air is used by the lungs when it exhales. That is why it can sing at such length without a stop: it has two breaths for every one it inhales.

FOUR

SEASONAL VISITORS

The call of the cuckoo is a nostalgic recollection of summer, of the sunny, fun-filled summers of youth. 'Letters to the Editor' indicate a competition between listeners, for the bird is less seen than heard, about the earliest call. As is fitting, this Kerry reader recorded a sighting and the call of the cuckoo in the first ever *Eye on Nature*: 'I saw the cuckoo here at Castlecove on March 31st, and Dan Galvin heard it sing on April 4th. "When the cuckoo sings on a leafless tree," the saying goes, "sell the cow and buy corn". But Dan Galvin says tradition has it that the cuckoo's early appearance means a spell of glorious weather. Take your choice!'[1] This was, in fact, a very early sighting. The cuckoo's usual time of arrival is in the second half of April, but there were 19th century reports of sightings as early as April 2nd and what was called 'an exceptionally early arrival' at Cape Clear on April 4th in 1969. In 1986, however, a cuckoo was officially authenticated at Wexford on March 18th.

A Dublin correspondent goes one better: 'In Stillorgan at 7.15am on March 5th, I heard a cuckoo call. The call seemed to be coming from the grounds of the St John of God hospital. All my hunting and fishing friends say that April and early May are the earliest the cuckoo has been heard in Ireland. But I know what I heard.'[2] Cuckoo calls in March have been notified to both *The Irish Times* and *The Times* of London, but to make the record official requires visual authentication. As one commentator on an early arrival said, the bird should be received '*cum grano salis*; which grain should be put on his tail that he may, if possible, be identified ... as a true bird or an unfeathered biped'.

There were letters describing the mobbing of a cuckoo by thrushes and pipits, as they tried to prevent her from laying in their nests. Several people saw young cuckoos being fed by a variety of birds: dunnock, blackbird and, exceptionally, a flock of small birds. 'While on holidays in late June in Connemara we saw an extraordinary thing. Just outside the house where we were staying was an ESB pole. Alerted by the noise, we looked out one day to see a gathering of small birds flying around in much agitation and seeming to feed and otherwise fuss over a cuckoo perched on the pole fittings. There were a dozen or more birds, with warblers among them. The commotion went on for about twenty minutes before the cuckoo moved to the corner of an old shed about one hundred yards away.'[3] Splendid views of cuckoo life are not uncommon in the open landscape of Connemara, and the late Tony Whilde, a fine naturalist, described a closely similar episode in *The Natural History of Connemara* (Immel, 1994). It was seen on the Sky Road, outside Clifden. 'Here, towards the end of July, eleven meadow pipits and one skylark were engaged in feeding one juvenile cuckoo which was perched on a fence post. Each small bird, in quick succession, perched briefly on the shoulder of the cuckoo, which turned its head sideways to accept the insect food from its hosts.'

Do cuckoos always and invariably leave the care of their young to other birds? There was a tantalising hint to the contrary: 'Uta Cogan of Long Island, off Schull, tells me she watched a pair of cuckoos lay in a thrushes' nest on Long Island, and then stick around and help feed the young cuckoo later on.'[4]

Compared with the competitive ritual of first cuckoos, the arrival of the swallow has sparked some delightfully spontaneous pleasure: it has attracted more letters than any other bird. 'Today (April 18th) I saw about twenty swallows at Whiting Bay, Co Waterford. I shouted a welcome to them and asked them about their journey, but they were busy enjoying the soft, misty day and the insects. Aren't they great!'[5] A great many people have swallows' nests in their sheds or garages, and are concerned if they do not arrive every year.

There were several reports of them at play: 'Two pairs of swallows nested this year in our shed, one pair in an old nest and the other in a fine new one. After the nest was built, and before either pair started to lay, we watched them at play one evening. One swallow would carry a hen feather while the other three gave chase. The first swallow would drop the feather and another would pick it up as it floated in the sky. This game went on for at least five minutes and they seemed to be enjoying themselves a great deal.'[6] Another correspondent saw a similar play. 'I have seen a swallow drop a feather, turn fifty yards away, catch it before it had fallen ten feet and repeat the trick five times.'[7]

The mobbing of cats has often been reported. 'Swallows swoop at cats when their fledglings are learning to fly, to distract their attention from young ones that might alight on the ground and not take off quickly enough.'[8] And: 'Last summer the swallows swooped at us. They were so aggressive that I could not go to the clothes line. The reason was that their fledglings were about to take to the air and were swaying on the side of the nest in our old hay-shed.'[9]

Swallows are not to be outdone by resident birds in eccentric locations for their nests. 'This year [1995] a swallow built a nest and hatched a clutch of chicks, all within fifteen inches of a large and very loud loudspeaker on Limerick Junction station. As stations go it is a busy one and every train gets about five announcements. Is there a record of a wild bird nesting in a noisier spot?'[10] They must, it seems, have escorted the fledglings out of the nest when the the trains were gone and the station was empty. Except at fledging time swallows seem impervious to human presence and, on this evidence, noise. On a visit to the Ulster History Park in Omagh we saw two nests a mere ten feet off the ground, inside the living area of the reconstructed Neolithic house. The swallows swooped in and out over the heads of the visitors.

House martins arrive, like the swallows, in early April and depart in August and September. They come to notice mainly because they build their mud-crafted nests under eaves of dwellings and most people welcome them. 'Since I moved into the country to a quiet residential area, I never see the mud nests of house martins on the eaves of any houses around me. When I see so many of them outside darting hither and thither, I wonder where can they be nesting?'[11] The answer is elsewhere, because the walls of new houses are usually too smoothly finished and paint-protected to provide a grip for the house martins' beakfuls of mud.

Sand martins nest in burrows in sand cliffs and in quarries, but one correspondent found them in a site that is quite special to Ireland. 'On a bog in Sligo I saw sand martins flying in and out of an old cutaway turf bank about three metres high. On a closer look I found that there were a dozen or more occupied nest-holes.'[12] This echoes descriptions of a century ago in *The Birds of Ireland*, by Richard Ussher and Robert Warren:

'Standing close to the face of a wall of peat, an old excavation some twelve feet high in the Co Tyrone, one may watch the numerous Sand-Martins fly in and out of their holes in it.' In an early *Eye on Nature*, one reader, who lives near a sand quarry where sand martins have nested for years, described a pre-migration gathering: 'On August 7th hundreds of them were flying overhead, like Alfred Hitchcock's *"The Birds"*. They were lining up on the electric wires in great numbers.'[13] Sand martins start leaving around the end of July.

Swifts are mainly associated with towns and cities, but only the antics of the Dublin swifts reached *Eye on Nature*. They were seen feasting on a nuptial flight of ants in Dartry[14] and nesting in a wrought iron vent over a door in Fitzwilliam Square.[15] They usually nest higher up, under eaves, but in the days when swifts swooped for flies around the heads of city horses, they nested quite commonly in holes beneath the window sills of Fitzwilliam's big Georgian houses. There was one report of an alpine swift at Killiney on March 19th 1992, a bird twice the weight of the common swift which sometimes flees out of Europe ahead of bad weather.[16]

Most migrant warblers are small, brown birds that are difficult to identify except by their song or call. The willow warbler has a sweet song but is outdone by the blackcap, and the chiffchaff has its own distinctive call. But the grasshopper warbler baffles many people. 'Near our house, during the latter part of May, a shrill vibratory sound could be heard at nightfall. Experts I have consulted consider it to be a cicada.'[17] A summer visitor from Africa, the grasshopper warbler now breeds in every county in Ireland. It is attracted to the tangled cover of young forestry, but its more traditional habitat is marshy ground with scrubby willows where it slips through the undergrowth like a mouse and trills almost ventriloquially, especially in the early hours of night. Sometimes it is mistaken for a corncrake: 'We were approaching the Leitrim moorings on the Ballyconnell Canal in early September when we were surprised to hear the call of a corncrake. We heard it four times as we passed rough land along the canal.'[18] The corncrake calls only during the breeding season in May and June. The grasshopper warbler often calls in September before it flies south.

Real corncrakes are now lamentably rare in Ireland, and have become the object of surveys and schemes to preserve their fast disappearing habitats. Records of their calling can be important. 'In June 1995, I heard a corncrake in the Suck valley for the first time in twelve years.'[19]

They arrive in April and may start calling while still on their way to traditional haunts. From mid-May to the end of July they are on their breeding grounds, mainly moist and uncut meadows, and early silage-making has hastened the great decline in their numbers. Bird societies ask farmers not to cut meadows in which corncrakes are nesting until after July and then to mow them from the centre outwards so that the families can escape. The water meadows of the Shannon callows house the only substantial numbers of corncrakes nowadays, with the odd *crex-crex* from old fields in Mayo and Donegal and on their islands. 'On September 10th [1995] I came across two corncrakes on the road to Roonagh Point in Co Mayo, one each side of the road. I watched them for a few minutes until they disappeared into the grass margin on their respective sides.'[20] Corncrakes stop calling in late July, and these two must have been getting ready to fly back to Africa.

'I have been fascinated this summer [1993] and last by a bird that spends its day perched on a larch branch about twelve feet above the ground, but every quarter to half minute darting off anything from two to twenty yards away and returning immediately. Obviously it is catching insects on the wing. Sometimes it is away for a quarter of a minute or so, presumably taking insects to its nest. It is about the size, shape and colour of a robin save that its breast is pale.'[21] It was a spotted flycatcher. These are migrants which arrive in spring, breed and fly back to South Africa in autumn. They can be very faithful to a nesting site. 'A pair of spotted flycatchers has nested in an artificial nest, an ornamental coconut husk in my shed for the sixth successive year. I feel sure they are the original pair that arrived in 1990, because each year they use the same positions in the trees surrounding the nest site.'[22] They could well be the same pair or, if not, some of their descendants. Birds rarely get the chance to die of old age, there are too many hazards on the way, but the oldest recorded flycatcher lived to be nine years of age.

Many of our winter migrants pass unnoticed, merely boosting the numbers of familiar resident species. Only the fieldfares and redwings catch the eye among flocks in the fields and hedgerows. Some strikingly different birds, however, can sometimes be watched from the living-room window, as flocks of waxwings descend on our gardens to devour cotoneaster berries and any others they can find. There are waxwing winters when thousands of birds come to visit: 1989 and 1996 were years of large 'irruptions', as this sort of mass-movement is called. 'On April 17th 1989, a flock of sixteen crested birds perched on the beech tree outside my house. They sang in trilling tones and were quite tame, allowing approach to about twenty five feet. They were somewhat larger and sturdier than a blackbird but had shorter tails. The outer half of the tail was dark except for a yellow band at the tip. The outer feathers of the wings were darker than the rest of the body and had red and yellow markings. I think they were waxwings.'[23] Waxwings are actually smaller than blackbirds but stubbier. When a population peak of these birds coincides with a shortage of rowan berries in the remote forests of Scandinavia and Siberia, the birds irrupt westward in winter, reaching Britain and the east coast of Ireland. As they arrive here when the various thrushes have stripped the berries from the bushes in the hedgerows, they tend to concentrate on gardens.

'On April 17th 1991, Linden Lea Park, Dublin, hosted a flock of about thirty waxwings, twittering and feeding in cotoneaster berries and the white petals of a blossoming cherry tree, and making little forays to a nearby gutter for water. Some of the birds fed each other with white petals, a charming sight.'[24] The end of April is an unusually late departure date for them. There were several reports in 1996: a flock of five in Clare that came in January and stayed until the end of March when they finished the berries in the host garden. There were two reports from north Dublin in mid-April, probably the same flock, which numbered thirty five according to observers.[25]

Between the appetites of birds and the decorations for Christmas, one would expect holly trees to lose most of their berries by mid-winter at the latest, but some well-laden trees seem, mysteriously to survive. 'Just outside our local post-office here in Rossinver, Co Leitrim, is a small holly tree, still sporting in the second week of April as many red berries as it did before Christmas. Is this a local phenomenon?'[26] A Killarney reader who keeps up with ornithological research had an explanation to offer: 'A 1984 study by B.K. and D.W. Snow in Britain showed that many adult mistle thrushes remain for the whole November-February period close to fruit-bearing trees or shrubs, particularly holly and hawthorn, which they vigorously defend from other thrushes. In normal winter weather they feed on earthworms, resorting to their food supply only when other food is unavailable. Here in Killarney one can still find a number of heavily-laden holly trees, presumably as a result of successful defence by mistle thrushes.'[27] As a rather distinctive native bird, one might expect the mistle thrush to be more widely known. But its large size and paler appearance, a bolder, upright stance, and an often quite yellow background to the strong markings on the breast can puzzle people, especially when mistle and song thrushes join up in flocks in late summer: 'Two or three times in August, and at the same time last year, a flock of birds have taken over my garden. They arrive in the evening, about fifty or sixty of them. They are quite big birds with thrush-like spotting on the breast, and the back has a clear herringbone pattern. On the second visit this year they had about twenty smaller birds with them, much darker and with thrush markings.'[28]

There are occasional reports of vagrant visitors that wander here from the continent. 'On April 4th we saw a hoopoe near Tramore and we were very glad to see him. Will he make his nest near Tramore?'[29] The beautiful hoopoe, with its crest like an Indian head-dress, is only a scarce, spring visitor to Ireland, mainly to the south coast. There have been no records of hoopoes nesting here, but birdwatchers keep hoping. Another hoopoe, well away from his usual Irish haunts, was seen, photographed and videoed in Colmanstown, an inland town in Co Galway.[30]

However, some exotic sightings are more likely to be escapes from captivity. A Mayo reader saw a cockatiel flying near his home and later found it dead and discovered that it was ringed.[31] This member of the parrot family, almost twice as big as a budgerigar, is a native of Australia and New Zealand and most certainly escaped from a cage.

'On October 21st, 1996, at about 9.50pm a neighbour and I saw what appeared to be a red-headed bunting on a telephone wire in Sandymount. The bird was vivid yellow with reddish-brown face and breast. It stayed for at least ten minutes constantly emitting a loud 'tweet' at a rate of about one per second.'[32] The appearance of the beautiful, red-headed bunting is unmistakable, and the description fits. It is a Central Asian resident which breeds from the Caspian Sea to north-west China, and a very rare vagrant to Europe. Most of the occasional sightings in this country have been regarded by experts as escapes from captivity, as they are imported into Britain as cage birds.

NOTES

FIVE

AND A PARTRIDGE IN A PEAR TREE

'As I shaved, I became aware of a peculiar, clamorous shrieking outside the window and was astonished to see one hundred to one hundred and fifty birds of all species, wren, blackbird, robin, crow, thrush, sparrow, flying erratically outside and close to the door of the yard. I came down quietly, opened it slightly and peeped out. On the ground outside was a hawk with a robin in its talons. It immediately dropped the robin and flew upwards through the circling mass of birds overhead. The robin preened its ruffled feathers and flew up to join his friends. Within five seconds there wasn't a bird in sight.'[1]

The mobbing of birds of prey by smaller species is quite frequent, but the number and variety involved in this instance was exceptional. The predator was probably a sparrowhawk, which is used to manoeuvring in confined spaces. Crows utter a special rasping note in the presence of hawks which would have added to the clamour. And the poor sparrowhawk went without its breakfast!

The sparrowhawk is the only hawk native to Ireland. Most of the letters about it have referred to mobbing, because the racket usually attracts attention. Almost invariably, human sympathy is directed towards the prey, usually small, attractive songbirds, as if the hawk was engaged in some unnatural act. But one correspondent appreciated the hawk's point of view: 'I have seen a sparrowhawk bring the life of a siskin, feeding on a nut bag, to an abrupt end. The hawk's actions were without malice or remorse, just another of nature's many and varied survival strategies.'[2]

They are also attentive parents. 'When on holidays at Lough Corrib, on hearing the call of a young hawk, I looked up to see an adult sparrowhawk flying quite slowly with a small bird or mouse in its claws.

The noisy youngster was flying about twenty feet below and slightly behind, when the parent bird released the tasty morsel which was expertly caught by the young bird.'[3] This feeding behaviour, which can be carried out by either parent, marks the final stage in the development of the young sparrowhawk before it becomes independent.

In most letters about sightings of kestrels they were confused with sparrowhawks, but there was no mistake about this one from a Co Galway nun. 'A visitor alighted on a little balcony outside my window. He was about a foot long and had plumage of a red-brick colour with a creamy-brown breast spotted like a thrush. With a stooped, sweeping turn of the head he looked in and his face was like an owl's, with a crooked bill. I was sorry when he took off and said to myself "Who says there is no God?" He was a beauty, that daring stranger.'[4]

Another correspondent paid close attention to a pair: 'In the last days of February I saw two kestrels hovering and gliding and circling one hundred feet or more up in the sky. They were making a shrill, high-pitched sound which seemed to drop about an octave at the end. My bird book says that their call note is a shrill *kee-kee-kee* while I thought that it dropped distinctly at the end.'[5] The kestrel also has a double note call described as *kee-lee* in the mating season.

Kestrels are falcons and belong to a different scientific order to the hawks. The latter join kites, harriers, vultures, buzzards and eagles in a separate order called accipiters. Falcons lack the powerful, spasmodic clutching mechanism in their talons by which accipiters kill their prey; they more usually kill by biting and severing the spine.

The European population of peregrine falcons was almost wiped out a few decades ago by organochlorine poisoning. DDT pesticides, used to kill insects, collected in the systems of insect-eating birds, which in turn were eaten by the peregrines. At quite a low concentration of the chemicals, the peregrines began to lay eggs with shells too thin to let the embryos survive. Widespread restraints on the use of DDT and dieldrin led to the recovery of peregrine populations, and Ireland's total of roughly four hundred breeding pairs is at the highest level for perhaps two centuries. With protection from persecution though the theft of young fledglings, or 'eyasses' for the falconry market continues, the effective control on their numbers is the availability of suitable nesting sites. Peregrine pairs have created new territories, especially in the east of

Ireland, around nests on quarry ledges, augmenting traditional sites on mountains and sea cliffs. 'Our school is lucky to have three pairs of peregrine falcons nesting in cliffs within a mile of us. They have only returned within the past couple of years. In our recent sightings the falcon, while hovering, is always surrounded by at least ten to twelve small birds and they seem to follow him around like the meadow pipit follows the cuckoo. Please don't give our location as we don't want the nest spoiled as happened here in the 'thirties and 'forties.'[6]

A defensive tactic used by flocking birds, from pigeons and starlings to gulls and rooks, is to bunch up tightly above or near the falcon. By stooping and feinting, the peregrine tries to make a bird break away from the flock, but it will not stoop into the mass of birds. 'In late August, from the railway bridge at Seapoint station, I was watching sea birds on the shoreline, when suddenly two oystercatchers let out warning cries which were taken up by all the other birds. All except the cormorants, who continued sunning their wings on the rocks, took off out to sea. At that moment the familiar shape of a falcon flashed by about four feet above the rocks and turned out to sea, picking up a flock of what looked like turnstones. It hit them as I have seen a peregrine hit pigeons in the Comeragh Mountains. How did the oystercatchers know to raise the alarm when they were facing the other way?'[7] Because oystercatchers are waders, and feed by probing the mud with their bills, their eyes are placed high on the side of the head, to spot danger from whichever side it comes.

The intimate lives of peregrines is rarely casually witnessed, but a specially keen observer in Co Clare watched a piece of family drama. 'I saw three young peregrines feeding off a rook on the ground with the parents supervising. As they attempted to take the food from each other, the young birds attracted the attention of a juvenile fox. He was attacked right away by both parents who bowled him over in three stoops, making hard contact with his back. I've seen them attack foxes before but did not realise they would inflict real damage. One of the parent foxes came later, but when she heard the aggressive calls of the parent falcons she was gone in a flash.'[8]

The merlin is the smallest of our falcons and usually glimpsed in rapid flight. It is relatively scarce in Ireland with less than two hundred pairs breeding on the island, generally away from habitation, so the following letter was highly unusual. 'A mysterious pair of birds nested with us this year, 1990, high up in a sycamore tree outside our kitchen door. The parents, larger than thrushes, would sit on a nearby electricity pole, keeping very still before flying off, silently and suddenly, to the fields or distant trees. They would arrive back with mice, frogs or bundles of worms, and pull them apart on the pole before approaching the nest, this with great caution and three or four stops to survey the scene.

"The male had a grey-blue back, with dark speckles on a light breast. The female had a brown head and back with a similarly speckled breast. Both had yellow legs, and their call sounded roughly like *qui-ik-ik*. They flew and hunted as a small bird of prey and sometimes were mobbed by the birds in a neighbouring rookery. Now that they have reared their two young and left, the swallows are back sitting and chatting on the electricity wires, and the small birds can help themselves to the oats that I scatter under the sycamore tree."[9]   These must have been exceptionally unobtrusive people, to have lived at such close quarters with a pair of merlins. The loss of heather from the hills due to overgrazing or land reclamation has been changing this falcon's nesting habits. In Northern Ireland, for example, merlins disappeared as ground nesters on moorland in the late 1970s but have been found since then nesting widely in trees, often in the abandoned nests of hooded crows.

The gyrfalcon, from arctic regions, occasionally visits the north-west of this country travelling from Greenland with flocks of barnacle geese, on which it preys. 'In spring I was delighted to see a gyrfalcon perched on a wall near the flock of barnacle geese, and I found two goose corpses stripped in the falcon manner. A significant number of records have been from the Mullet peninsula, opposite the Iniskeas, so the link with the wintering barnacles is probably of long standing.'[10] Another visitor from the arctic wilderness visited Donegal: 'In April 1994, I saw a snowy owl where the road crosses a piece of bog land near the Lackagh River.'[11]

There were reports of buzzards from Donegal, but the only other native raptor reported by *Eye on Nature* correspondents is the hen harrier, of which about three hundred pairs breed on moorland, mountains and in conifer forests. 'Recently I came across a large hawk which I did not recognise. It had rounded wings and was covering a corn field in a very easy-going fashion. It was a reddish-brown and had a distinctive white patch across the rump.'[12]   It was almost certainly a female hen harrier, which hunts over agricultural land and lives on small mammals and birds.

Another bird of prey, the barn owl, is also in decline here. A denizen of the dark, it flits like a pale, silent ghost about the countryside and so is not often observed. There are various reasons given for its decline: eating poisoned rats and mice, rodents form sixty-five percent of its diet here, changing farm practices and buildings, and now a Co Mayo ornithologist, Martin Zajac of Killala, suggests that the weather may play a part. 'As a bird with worldwide distribution, and mostly at home in the tropics, it would suffer from severe weather on the northern edge of its range. Although we have very little snow cover in Ireland, I think that very wet and windy weather also affects a barn owl's hunting success. Dutch barns of the old, close-in type were especially important, not only as nesting sites but also as a place to hunt in harsh weather when there was an influx of rodents. It is my belief that birds in such barns are a nucleus that keep the population going in a run of bad winters.'[13] Colin Shawyers' study for the Hawk Trust shows that the barn owl's choice of nest site is, indeed, related to rainfall. Over eighty percent of known nest sites in Ireland are in buildings, compared with sixty-five percent in England's drier climate.

Many of the game birds that were plentiful in the wild, in fields, in woodland and on the heather-covered mountains, have virtually disappeared and their place has been taken by birds that have been hand-reared and released. 'Our cotoneaster, which is about six feet high and thirty feet from the back door, was laden with red berries until last week when five or six pheasants landed on it and stripped it completely of berries.'[14] Cotoneaster berries, like rowan and hawthorn, are attractive to many birds; but the pheasants must have been hand-reared to come so close to the house.

Grey partridge are being reintroduced in Co Offaly on a wilderness created by Bord na Mona and local communities on cutaway bog. One would be forgiven for thinking that Wales is more hospitable to declining species, judging from the following letter: 'We stayed with a relative in Wales, whose house overlooks Tregaron Bog, home of kites, the occasional osprey, and even a bittern. The most surprising thing for me was to see a partridge sitting on the roof of the house when we arrived. It was not the slightest disturbed by the banging of car doors, but only gazed down on us with mild interest, and was presently joined by its mate. Apparently they are constantly there and pay little attention to pheasant shooting nearby.'[15]

The midlands are also host to another extremely scarce game bird, the tiny quail. In 1989, which was a good year for the bird, a Kildare farmer 'flushed a bevy of half-a-dozen sparrow-sized young quail' in his spring barley in August;[16] and its distinctive call, *kwit-kwit-wit*, was also heard in Waterford, Wexford and Sligo. In June 1995 a Westport correspondent heard one calling, on two separate occasions, from grassland outside the town.[17]

Occasionally letters record rare or mysterious game-birds. The red-legged partridge that visited Kilmurry graveyard, near Crossmolina, must have escaped or have survived from a release programme. 'It hung about for up to three hours and was fed crumbs at a distance of three feet, any closer and she moved away. Nobody had ever seen such a bird before.'[18] Another mysterious bird might or might not have been a ptarmigan, a grouse of the high mountains, resident in Scotland: 'At about 6.30pm on August 25th [1988], while driving a narrow country road a mile or so south of Roscrea, Co Tipperary, I came upon an all-white bird standing beside the road. I pulled up beside it and it examined me and my car with interest. It had a short, pink stripe on the crown of its head and its legs were so covered with feathers that I could not see its feet. It was approximately dove-like in shape and size, and when it eventually flew off it had a completely jet-black, fan-like tail. From my bird book this looked as if it should be a ptarmigan, but I did not think these were found in Ireland. Could it have been (i) an escaped pet, (ii) a bird blown off course, (iii) a bird brought in by a gun club? In the nearby Slieve Bloom mountains are notices restricting the shooting of grouse.'[19] A ptarmigan is certainly the best fit, although in August the back should still be a mottled grey; it turns white only in winter. If it was a gun club release, nobody owned up.

SIX

WILD CALLS IN THE SKY

The largest Irish birds, indeed, the biggest that take to the wing anywhere, command special concern for their welfare from human neighbours in the cities. 'All through the summer [1989] I have been watching a family of swans, two adults and five cygnets, on the River Liffey between Chapelizod and Islandbridge. I have lived close to the Liffey all my life and cannot ever remember seeing as many as five cygnets surviving right through until they were almost fully grown.'[1] This pair of swans, which had bred for years on the same stretch of the Liffey, was studied by the ornithologist Richard Collins. They had, in fact, hatched eight eggs that year, but lost three of the cygnets between the end of May and early July. Accidents are due to local hazards such as strong currents through weir and culverts, getting hit by oars, tangled in discarded fishing tackle or stoned by vandals.

'Recently on the busy Ennis-Limerick bypass I saw a common but heart-lifting sight. A male mute swan stood in the middle of the thoroughfare while motorists slowed to a halt. Once the swan gave the all-clear his missus emerged from the bushes followed by eight cygnets in single file, and all crossed safely to the water meadows. The motorists all had the idiotic smiles of proud grandparents!'[2]

Whooper and Bewick swans are winter visitors which arrive here in October and stay until March or April. The resonant contact-call of the whoopers draws the eye to the classic V of their flight-formation. 'There are more than two hundred swans on Keel Lake, Achill, why do they only seem to call or whoop in calm, frosty weather?'[3] These were whooper swans which had just arrived from Iceland. They can be heard better in calm, frosty weather, and at night.

39

The migrations of large birds impinge on our consciousness often through these call-of-the-wild vocalisations. 'Very late on April 21st, my friend and I heard an amazing honking and goose-like sound. Very high against the clear night sky we saw a V-shaped skein of what must have been hundreds of birds.'[4] They were either white-fronted or greylag geese returning to Iceland and Greenland. Thousands of white-fronted geese winter on the Wexford Slobs, and hundreds of greylag geese winter on Poulaphouca Reservoir and Broad Lough in Wicklow from October until April.

A very large number of barnacle geese, between seven and eight thousand, winter in Ireland from their breeding grounds in north-east Greenland. They settle mainly on the coast and on islands offshore, and the greatest concentration is on the Iniskea Islands off north Mayo. One observer found some further inland. 'On February 15th I saw a very large flock of seventy-two whooper and Bewick swans and, in the midst of them, nine barnacle geese. They were all grazing greedily on fresh grass growing in a water meadow between Ballinamore and Ballyconnell. I think this may be a first record for barnacles in Leitrim, eighty kilometres from the sea.'[5] The nearest large wintering colony would be Lissadell, on the shore of Sligo Bay.

Brent geese, the smallest of the wild geese, come in their thousands from their breeding grounds in arctic Canada and Greenland to coastal sites in Ireland. Strangford Lough, the North Bull in Dublin and Tralee Bay are their main sites, but smaller flocks also come to other locations. 'In a miserable, rainy nor'-westerly gale on October 6th [1989], I saw four Brent geese heading for Trabreaga Bay just half-a-mile from my house in Carndonagh, Co Donegal. There are usually about two hundred to two hundred and fifty Brent and barnacle geese in the Bay each winter, and I always look forward to their arrival. They usually come from the end of October to mid-November, and I have never seen them this early before.'[6]

'On September 19th 1994, walking along the causeway leading to the Bull Island, I noticed ten Brent geese landing on the water. Brent geese are regular visitors in their hundreds to the Bull Island, but I never before saw them as early as September.'[7] The first Brent geese arrive in Kerry and Strangford Lough in late August, but the main migration is in September and October. The Bull Island birds usually make a first stop at Strangford Lough.

Most correspondents are surprised at the aggressive behaviour of mallard drakes, and are astonished to hear that rape often occurs in the flock. 'In St Stephen's Green I saw two male mallards attacking a female, who seemed to be the mother of a couple of ducklings, chasing her quite aggressively about the pond. At one stage she scurried across the water, towards where I was, chased by the two males, and suddenly dived underneath to escape them. I watched carefully to see where she resurfaced, but she didn't.'[8] And 'In the main pond at Bushy Park there are about thirty to forty mallard ducks and twice the number of drakes, a fairly constant proportion at all times. We have noticed the same preponderance of drakes on the ponds of the Dodder; there are usually about forty to fifty ducklings swimming around with their parents. This year, we have only seen one family of four and another of two although the parents seem to have finished nesting.'[9]

The mallard drake is a beautifully coloured bird and in most populations males are in the majority. More males are hatched, and there is a higher rate of mortality among females at breeding time, when they can be gang-raped by the extra males and often drowned in the fray. The preponderance of males thus leads to low breeding success. In natural marshy areas, breeding females space themselves out in accessible feeding areas, away from the males. But on park lakes and ponds they are in a confined space and so are vulnerable to male attack.

The shelduck is an equally handsome bird, found in all coastal regions, feeding in flocks on the ebbing tide. At the beginning of the breeding season shelducks separate into pairs, and a pair arrives every year at the channel of a small river on our strand, to nest in a nearby rabbit burrow. One shelduck family stopped the traffic near Kinsale bridge in June: 'We came around a bend to find two parent shelduck with a tiny duckling walking in close order, single file, in front of the car. We proceeded about one hundred yards up the road, amid continuous quacking, and, on rounding the next bend, came on a lay-by where the remainder of the family, seven ducklings, were 'parked' and waiting in a tight group. The reunited family calmly proceeded towards the water, ignoring the fascinated motorists, halted to let them pass.'[10] One interesting fact about shelduck: in July most of the adults leave a few nannies to mind the still very young families, and fly off to the mouth of the Elbe in Germany to moult. Over 100,000 of them congregate there in the sandbanks of the

Grosser Knechtsand.

The only teal that has made an appearance in *Eye on Nature* was in the jaws of a Welsh stoat. 'When the stoat saw me he retreated and the teal jumped into the river and swam towards the other bank. The stoat returned in search of his prey, cast about, stood on his hind legs and saw it, then followed it, swimming strongly. He grabbed the teal and disappeared into the long grass.'[11]

Populations of duck fluctuate from time to time in their various territories, or redistribute themselves between them. A fisherman on Lough Corrib noted the increase in the common scoter, a dark sea duck with a small Irish breeding population: 'Ten years ago there were one or two pairs in the Oughterard area, now [1994] there are one or two pairs on every island.'[12] Common scoter are mostly winter visitors from arctic Finland and Russia, but about one hundred pairs have been breeding on large inland lakes. 'For two days in early August I saw a diving duck on Lough Corrib with twenty-three ducklings in tow. The sight was also witnessed by some friends. None of us had ever seen so many ducklings in one family.'[13] Amalgamation of broods takes place in two species of duck, the common scoter and the red-breasted merganser, perhaps to let the female moult.

An unidentified flock of birds in Dublin Bay, might also have been scoters. 'Looking over Scotsman's Bay in Sandycove in January and early February I noticed about one hundred and fifty yards out small groups (15-50) of dark birds moving south in V-formation approximately a foot above the waves.'[14] Common scoter usually behave in this manner, flying in both large and small flocks just above the water in a line. Large flocks winter on the Co Louth coast, but flocks of several hundred have been seen at Skerries and Portmarnock. Kells Bay in Co Kerry has given the highest counts in Ireland, some seven thousand in January of 1996.

The coot, another dweller in ponds, lakes and rivers, would seem a nervous and inoffensive little fellow. Not so, according to one correspondent. 'Forget Ballymun, the 'Family' is alive and well and living in Phoenix Park. Charlo the Coot cleared the Furry Glen of all other coots and most other birds to raise his own family of three, with two survivors. He built several holiday homes all round the lake, and then hunted his two kids mercilessly away so that he could start a second brood. Now there are five, and one of them is already learning to chase ducks and moorhens. As July turned into August, eight or ten ducks, a brood of four moorhen chicks and a couple of little red diver birds, dabchicks or little grebes, had somehow weathered the coot storm, not to mention, magpies, jays and a heron.'[15]

Herons are the most spectacular of the birds associated with water, and inspired almost as many letters as the magpies. They patrol the suburbs between the rivers and reservoirs of south Dublin and the coastline with great regularity, inspecting garden ponds on the way. One heron brought regularity to a fine art: 'Here in Killiney we have a barren, shingle shore except at low spring water when rocks, seaweed, pools, etc, are revealed. Without fail the heron then appears, occasionally two, and sets about catching crabs. He takes his time breaking them up in his bill before gulping them down. How do they know that it is low tide on Killiney beach when to my knowledge there is no heronry nearby? I've never seen them patrolling to see the state of the tide. Do they observe the phases of the moon?'[16] They may, who knows? But they do maintain a regular beat. They can, however, take advantage of what one correspondent calls 'a window of opportunity'.

'Herons have always stalked the banks of the river in Newport, Co Mayo, a superb fishery. In the late 1980s the Co Council floodlit the town's two handsome, cut-stone bridges, and the herons can fish through the night in mid-summer glow. Soon after, at Easter, we watched from the shadows while a heron stood centre stage in the middle of the river, stalking the sea trout returning to sea after spawning. It was still a learning process. It took him two nights to figure out that while trout will go to sea in large numbers on the lip of a falling tide, they will not take the same risks on a rising tide. And so he stood, like a silver-grey ghost in the river, his beak undipped, while the water rose about him. On the third night he wasn't there and we imagined him snoring quietly in the heronry above the town, waiting for another window of opportunity.'[17]

A further example of opportunism was recorded by another reader: 'I watched a heron in the River Nanny waiting patiently to catch his breakfast. Suddenly it dashed frantically along the river for about twenty metres and just as suddenly stopped. This continued for some time on both sides of the river. Then I noticed that its movements were synchronised with the diving and surfacing of a cormorant. As the cormorant dived in the middle of the river and swam up-stream, the heron ran along the side, presumably hoping to avail of the cormorant's efforts as fish would flee to the sides and come within his reach.'[18]

Although herons eat a variety of food, they prefer fish or eels, but in a pinch they will eat frogs, small mammals, crustaceans, insects, worms and even birds. 'Early one morning in November I spotted a heron trying to swallow what I first thought was a rat but turned out to be a bird. He was dipping it in and out of a pool and attempting to swallow it. At one stage all that was visible were the wings. When he could get no further he would regurgitate it and start all over again. After several attempts he succeeded and the last thing I saw disappear down the heron's gullet were the legs.'[19]

An elegant cousin of the heron is the Mediterranean's little egret, which, twenty-five years ago, was still a glamorous rarity for Irish bird-watchers. Then came a succession of influxes to the south coast, with birds staying for longer and longer periods. The Saleen estuary, a muddy, leafy estuary off Cork Harbour, with trees for egrets to roost in, has been a favoured wintering-ground since 1992, and a reader saw a heron, in September, 1995, trying to drive two new egret arrivals from its territory.[20] The influx of whole groups of egrets to southern lagoons, part of a general expansion by the bird and perhaps related to global warming, has encouraged the hope that egrets will soon be breeding here. There have been records from most coastal counties, including those in letters to *Eye on Nature* which placed egrets near Louisburgh[21] in December 1993 and near Portmarnock[22] in February 1997. The little egret is a pure white bird, 'a purer white than the surrounding snows' as described by one observer in March 1995.[23] In the breeding season it has stylish plumes, for which it was hunted in former times to decorate millinery.

The call of the curlew, soundtracked on a commercial for Harp lager, led one of our neighbours to call it 'the Sally O'Brien bird'. In *Eye on Nature* the curlew lived up to its advertising reputation for inducing nostalgia for home and girlfriends. One expatriate met, as regular companions, reminding him of home, 'the curlews with their lovely call on the strand at Al Khabar, Saudi Arabia, in an air temperature of one hundred and ten degrees, not once but regularly throughout the year'.[24] These birds were member of the Siberian family, *Numenius arquate orientalis*, which winter on the Red Sea and the Persian Gulf.

Curlews forage usually on mudflats and salt marshes, probing with their long bills and feeding by both sight and touch on insects, worms and small bivalves. In the breeding season they move to moorland and farmland, nesting on the ground in shallow depressions. 'On May 8th, seven curlews appeared in our back garden and remained for a couple of weeks, feeding constantly from dawn to dusk on worms. On some days there were thirteen. Our back garden is a marshy field near Ardnacrusha Canal.'[25] Breeding curlews may feed in groups, with the male bird relieving the nesting female to allow her to go to the feeding ground. If they are nesting on moorland they are more solitary. It is unusual for them to feed so close to houses, although a Dublin reader saw a flock of curlews feeding on a school playing pitch in Ranelagh in November and December.[26]

Smaller cousin of the curlew, the whimbrel is more usually a bird of passage, seen along our shores on its journey between wintering sites in Africa and breeding grounds in Iceland. The Shannon callows, too, see a constant traffic of whimbrels in late April and May, as small parties stop to feed in the moist grasslands on their migration north. One whimbrel travelling up the east coast did not make it to Iceland in spring of 1996: 'I was walking down Leinster Road, Rathmines, when I saw a magpie dive-bombing another bird of about equal size, brown and cream in colour, which seemed to have a broken wing. I rescued it and made a nest for it in a dense hedge away from predators. It appeared to be a woodcock as it had a snipe-like beak and long legs with black claws, also very long.'[27] It was more likely to be a whimbrel which, unlike the woodcock, has long black legs and feet. It may have been wounded by a peregrine, or by flying into cables on its spring migration, and the magpie was just being opportunistic.

Among the waders feeding along the shore in winter, the noisy oystercatchers, with their long orange bills, are quick to catch the eye. 'Looking at a group of about eight oystercatchers on Carlingford Lough, I was surprised to see that two birds had only one leg each. Even with binoculars I could see no "stump" or other sign of damage in either bird. When the group moved off the two hopped along in a rather comical fashion, but were well able to keep up. Over the following four or five days I failed to see them again and my guess was that they had not survived.'[28] Shorebirds such as oystercatchers and gulls often 'snooze' on one leg, the other raised tightly to the body, sometimes for warmth in frosty weather. When disturbed in this mode, oystercatchers can hop along on one leg, not bothering to put down the other unless their equilibrium is disturbed; indeed, they are the only waders that hop.

Some exotic visiting waders are reported each year. English visitors saw a black-winged stilt at Our Lady's Island in Wexford,[29] and two little girls saw six avocets beside the causeway to Bull Island on an Irish Wildbird Conservancy open day.[30] The black-tailed godwit is a regular winter visitor from Iceland to all coastal areas but rarely breeds here. However, there were two observations of it in breeding plumage here in 1991: one of a flock at Rosscarbery, Co Cork in July,[31] and another of a flock at the mouth of Oranmore Bay, Co Galway, in the same month.[32]

The drumming of the snipe, rather than its call, a harsh '*creech*', when disturbed, engages most readers. 'What is the bird that we hear during March and April at dusk in a small bog nearby? I would describe it as the sound which might be produced by blowing through a long pipe while rapidly closing and releasing the wind with the palm of the hand. There might be ten or twelve such sounds, beginning rather softly, getting louder, and then soft towards the end. The call seems to be made while the bird is marking out territory, almost, in fact, encircling us. Once we heard an answering call, on a higher and slightly thinner tone. We have never seen the bird.'[33] The drumming of the snipe is actually a non-vocal sound made by the male as part of territorial and mating display. He encircles and stakes out his territory by rising about one hundred metres into the air and diving at an angle of forty-five degrees with his tail feathers spread out. The sound is caused by the wind vibrating through these feathers. The female's response is a vocal call which sounds like *chip-er-chip-er-chip-er*.

A northern reader had another name for the snipe, borrowed from the sound of drumming: 'When I was a boy living in the country in Co Antrim, the drumming of the male snipe and the response of the female were familiar and much loved sounds of spring and early summer. Locally the male snipe was called the heather-bleat and the female the cut-peat, names suggestive of the sounds associated with them.'[34] Another letter referred to the male snipe as the 'minnie-gower'[35] which is a corruption of the Irish name *mionnán gabhar*, literally a goat kid because that is what the sound resembles.

SEVEN

BIRDS AT THE TIDE

 At the interface of land and sea, aggression and piracy seem to take on a shriller note, and the thuggish behaviour of gulls engaged some correspondents. 'The peace of the tidal area of the Dodder was shattered when dozens of gulls and rooks mobbed a heron, who flapped and croaked until he was driven up and away over the Lansdowne Road east stand.'[1]

Skirmishes between gulls and herons are quite frequent. Mobbing behaviour in birds is very infectious and often draws several species. Sometimes it is mobbing of a predator or a feeding competitor, but at other times it is a practice which scientists call klepto-parasitism: harassing another to steal its food. 'I was observing wildlife on the rocky foreshore between Dun Laoghaire and Sandycove when I saw a vicious attack by six or seven gulls on a seal. They continuously swooped, shrieked and dived above its exposed head. When nose-diving they always levelled off a few feet above the seal and never made contact with their target. Eventually the seal disappeared and resurfaced further away and the gulls lost sight of it.

'On another occasion I saw a similar number of gulls harassing a heron in a very vicious air attack. The heron was obviously terrified as it swerved in all directions from the all-points swooping of the shrieking gulls. Finally the heron flew as fast as it could out to sea with the gulls right on its tail until I lost sight of them beyond Sandycove. Perhaps the heron had swallowed a fish and the gulls were trying to make it regurgitate it.'[2]

In contrast we had some 'educated' birds: 'I was walking by New Square in Trinity College when I saw a pair of herring gulls standing close together on the grass. What drew my eye to them was the fact that their feet were moving rapidly and they were not moving anywhere. Then I saw one leaning over and snapping its bill in the grass and realised that this curious behaviour was a feeding ploy. Herring gulls attending university appear quite smart and sophisticated as their foot-tapping brings a prompt reward of dinner.'[3]

Herring gulls often move inland to feed on farm land and municipal dumps, but some readers were surprised to see cormorants away from the sea. 'I was astonished to see a cormorant, in my experience a timid bird of the seashore and tidal rivers, floating downstream on the River Arra, a tributary of the River Deel. It looked in no way lost or bedraggled.'[4] Outside the breeding season, cormorants are now quite common birds inland in Ireland on lakes and wetlands, where they feed on coarse fish, especially in winter.

'In September and early October I observed a pair of shags or cormorants flying back and forth between the Gravel Pit Lake, near my house, and Trawbreaga Bay about half-a-mile away. In mid-October I saw the same birds and was surprised to see a juvenile swimming and diving in the lake.'[5] These birds were cormorants and it is not unusual for them to nest in trees at inland lakes; shags are exclusively marine birds. For the first month or so of their lives, young cormorants are fed by their parents with regurgitated fish, and the pair could still be feeding a juvenile at the end of September.

'Recently I noticed an early morning flight of up to forty cormorants flying south through Dalkey Sound. In the evening, just before dark, they return in V-formation. We never see them fishing in groups.'[6] Cormorants have communal roosting sites; they flock together on the rocks, grooming, airing their oxters and stretching their wings or, as some research suggests, to reduce body temperature. But they fish separately, dispersed over the sea.

Among the most attractive summer visitors to our shores are the terns, with their angular wings and swooping flight. Sandwich, roseate, little and common terns come to Ireland to breed from winter quarters in West Africa. Arctic terns, on the other hand, spend the winter on the pack-ice of the Antarctic, but travel a round trip of up to twenty thousand miles each year to breed in these islands and as far north as Greenland and Iceland.

'On a beach near Louisburgh I saw a pair of small sea birds very like terns but much smaller than those I usually see. They were flying up and down a channel and screeching at me.'[7] These were our local, little terns which were nesting nearby. They like to nest in small colonies on shingle beaches that also appeal to people, and as they are already very susceptible to predation and unseasonable storms, this extra disturbance affects their breeding results. They have declined to fewer than two hundred pairs in Ireland, and on the east coast Birdwatch Ireland, formerly the Irish Wildbird Conservancy, takes special steps to guard their breeding areas: at Kilcoole, Co Wicklow, even a many-stranded electric fence to keep the foxes away.

Set against great ocean distances, the journey from seashore to our inland lakes is trivial, especially for birds well used to using fresh water on their Arctic breeding grounds. 'On November 26th I came upon an injured great northern diver on the banks of the canal leading into the Shannon. I returned next day to find the bird dead, and a friend confirmed the identification. How does one account for a sea bird turning up in the centre of Ireland?'[8] Great northern divers, wintering here from the Arctic, are predominantly birds of the coastline, but they are seen occasionally fishing on the large western lakes.

While many sea-birds, like gulls, terns and cormorants, are coastal birds, many other sea birds live most of their lives at sea and only come to islands or isolated cliffs on the mainland to breed. Gannets, puffins, little auks, razorbills, storm petrels and shearwaters, are rarely seen unless they are beached, injured or dead, and corpses give a better and more lasting visual impression, and a better opportunity for inspection of the bird, than any photograph.

In *Another Life,* Michael once described gannets fishing off the rocks at the end of the strand: 'shellbursts in the sea just beyond the breakers'. Gannets, he wrote, 'are the Concordes of our sea birds. The big spear of a beak is pointed imperiously ahead of a body the size of a goose, the narrow, albatross wings spread stiffly out across six feet of air. The eyes face forward, like our own, to give acute, binocular vision. Watching from Slea Head beyond Dingle, we have seen them dropping vertically from their maximum height of about one hundred and forty feet. But here, in a more intimate arena, preying on a shoal of something swimming in a vortex of the tide, their plunges were almost casual, slanting down on half-closed wings from a mere thirty or forty feet. Still, such velocity into shallow water, at times into the broken surf itself, made us wonder about their hidden trajectory and their specially strengthened skulls.'

This brought a very interesting letter to *Eye on Nature.* 'Your description of gannets diving at a slant into shallow water reminds me of what an old Inishmurray fisherman once told me. He says the gannet dives perpendicularly, "straight as a pin", on *herring*, which swim horizontally, but at an angle on *mackerel* which "play" with their heads downward and tails breaking the surface. The islanders fished herring but not mackerel commercially, so the gannets' method of diving decided whether or not they put to sea in pursuit of the shoal.'[9]

But their decisive and relentless plunge sometimes lands them in hidden dangers. 'Driving along Inch Strand in Co Kerry, we found a gannet caught in a portion of net. There was another gannet in the net but it was dead. In trying to release the bird it tried to bite us, but I put a coat over its head and, with the help of another man, we succeeded in cutting the net from its neck and feet. It was weak, but managed to flap its way to the water's edge. About a mile further along the beach we came on another gannet in a similar plight. We cut away the strings from its throat and body, and it ran towards the water. I suspect these birds were caught in torn portions of net which had been thrown away by fishermen. They had been washed up by a high tide.'[10] Fishermen, please note.

Sometimes the elements are too robust for the smaller sea birds. 'My neighbours found a little auk during the recent gales, struggling to get back on to the beach at Derrynane Bay. However, every time it got to the high ground overlooking the beach, it was blown back across the sand-dunes. It was exhausted and easy to catch and, after offering it water and strips of fish, which it refused, we put it in a large pool. Suddenly, to our delight, it took to the air, circled a bit and flew off. Its flight was strong and purposeful, yet it had seemed so exhausted on the ground and could only struggle fitfully along, flapping its wings. Were its legs weak because it is pelagic?'[11] The little auk, not much bigger than a starling, spends the winter some distance off the coast, particularly off the south-west, but is sometimes blown into land in storms. Up to a dozen single birds are found dead each year, but in the last 'wreck' in 1950 about fifty were picked up in Cork and a dozen were found in a field in Carlow.

All the auks, razorbills, puffins, guillemots and little auks, move clumsily on land because their legs are set far back, to facilitate diving for food. This makes them waddle like penguins; indeed, the great auk, extinct since the middle of the nineteenth century, has been described as a northern equivalent of the penguin. 'On January 3rd we were surprised to see a small penguin on the beach at Greencastle. It seemed quite fit and content, showing no fear as we approached to within two yards of it. After about three-quarters of an hour preening, it swam away. Might it have escaped from some zoo?'[12] The small penguin was almost certainly a storm-stressed razorbill, briefly ashore.

Another auk, the puffin, is that engaging little bird with an extraordinary, triangular, brightly coloured beak that enables it to carry bundles of sand eels, draped crossways, to its young. It lives at sea and only comes to the coast to breed on islands and remote mainland cliffs, where it usually nests in burrows excavated in soft ground. Some puffins off the Antrim coast found a local, handy take-away.

'When we started our salmon farm off the Antrim coast, we noticed almost immediately an increase in bird and sea life in the area. The first year's high point was a visit from a basking shark. But the most intriguing observation is the seeming return to the area of the puffins. One of our colleagues is a local fisherman who knows the coast intimately. He does not remember seeing puffins since the 1930s when he was a boy. Recently we have noticed puffins in the vicinity of our net pens, which are high-seas Bridgestones moored about a mile out to sea. Would they possibly be attracted by the sand eels which tend to accumulate against out nets on the uptide side at certain times?'[13] This seems very likely, and the birds may well have travelled up from the small puffin colonies breeding off Island Magee, a dozen miles down the coast.

Two other ocean-going birds that have made an appearance in *Eye on Nature* are the storm petrel and the Manx shearwater, both of which nest in burrows and crevices on some of our remoter islands. 'In October on the ferry from Rosslare to La Havre we found late in the evening a little storm petrel sitting in a doorway leading to the deck. It was apparently resting from the strong winds. We kept it in our cabin for a while, but after half-an-hour it started flying, and we brought it out on deck again where it took off into the stormy night. Was it on its way migrating south, or do storm petrels stay all year around, and is anything known about their numbers?'[14] In October the storm petrels were leaving their breeding ground in Ireland and Britain and moving out to the open sea. Ireland has the largest breeding population in the world, difficult to assess, since the birds come ashore only at night, but put at somewhere between fifty and one hundred thousand pairs. Most birds migrate south for the winter to the warmer waters off the western and southern coasts of Africa.

Although the Manx shearwater normally lives far out in the Atlantic, one turned up in Connacht. 'In May I was fishing in Lough Corrib and gulls were feeding on the mayfly. I saw what I took to be a kestrel picking mayfly from the surface of the lake. It was completely dark on top and whitish underneath with kestrel-shaped wings, and it flew in bursts of five to six wing beats then a glide. When I got closer to it I saw that it was a Manx shearwater.'[15] These birds are sometimes seen on inland lakes, and if this one was really feeding on mayfly it raises an interesting question, because their normal diet is small fish and molluscs.

Letters and phone calls come regularly to *Eye on Nature* looking for guidance on the care of orphaned or injured birds. 'We found a young ringed plover sitting all alone on the beach. At first we thought it was dead but when we went closer it ran off very quickly over the stones. We caught it and brought it home. Next day I got up early to catch sandhoppers for it which it ate greedily. When it had eaten the lot we decided to let it go on the beach. It ran off for a while and then froze. We took it to where a flock of ringed plovers were feeding at seaweed; it ran over to them and they all walked off together.'[16]

Orphans are not always what they seem, and little birds shamming dead may be waiting for their mothers. It is best to go right away for about an hour or two and then see if the bird is still in trouble. Take it home only with the intention of releasing it back into the wild as soon as it can fend for itself. Feeding a chick is an enormous commitment. Fly-eating chicks, such as wrens, swallows or house martins need ten flies every half-hour, fed with a tweezers. Later, the flies must be dangled on the end of a thread to teach the bird to catch food on the wing. All this is a daunting undertaking. Similar dedication is needed for worm-eating birds; the seed-eaters are easier to care for, but they, too, must be fed roughly every half-hour with ground-up seeds or cereal baby-foods. And there are many life-supporting routines, such as preening, that parent birds teach their young and we can do nothing about.

Injured birds are another matter. Superficial wounds can be cleaned and disinfected, and if the bird is in shock, say, mauled by the cat, it should be kept in a dark, well-ventilated box in a warm and quiet place for about an hour. It can be difficult to set tiny, broken bones and the job should be left to a veterinary surgeon.

EIGHT

FEARLESS ON THE LAWN

Because of their very numbers and their ubiquity in our lives, birds get a lot of our casual attention, but furry animals seem to have first claim on our affection. Even in a country of such strong farming traditions and prejudices, the fox still has many friends. 'During the year 1990 I was fortunate in spotting two beautiful foxes in the wild. So I was very disappointed to find some time later two dead foxes within a mile of each other; both had their tails missing. Is there a bounty for such slaughter.'[1]

'It is the opinion of all wildlife biologists,' the zoologist James Fairley wrote bluntly in his *Irish Beast Book*, 'that bounties are a wicked waste of time and money'. Thus, no official bounties exist now, but gun clubs and farmers have been reintroducing competitions for fox kills, and the brushes are necessary to win the prize. Gun clubs blame foxes for the decline in the number of game birds such as pheasant; while farmers see them as predators on lambs. Fox experts say that foxes are 'decreed by nature to cull the weak, sick or dying'; and they are scavengers as well as predators and often feed on sheep's afterbirth and the milky droppings of lambs. Many of the lambs found at fox dens were dead or dying when the fox collected them.[2] Shooting does not reduce the number of foxes in a locality; as with most animals, it is the availability of food that determines the population. All animals produce surplus young to allow for predation.

Our neighbourhood fox or foxes patrol all the local hen houses hoping for dereliction on the part of owners. We lost our hens to them one night when we forgot to close them in. Our fault! Birds are a welcome food item when they can get them, but foxes dine predominantly on beetles and earthworms, on fruit in season and on any carrion they can find. 'I once watched a fox digging in the sand banks near spring low-water mark on the channel of inner Dundrum Bay, in Co Down. It was digging for sand eels which were spawning in the sand in large numbers. It is generally accepted that foxes are opportunistic feeders and will scavenge on the tide-line where they can.'[3] We often follow the fox-tracks along the tide-line on our strand.

Their new champions are city dwellers, who are delighted to see a fox, preferably with cubs, in the back garden. From Blackrock where the foxes have territories: 'I have often seen one or two parent foxes striding across the lawn at night with perhaps three cubs scampering behind. I think the fox is absolutely magical; its cry in the night is magnificent.'[4] And in the heart of the city: 'On New Year's Eve at 1.18am, while returning from a party, I saw a fox in Raglan Road, the first sighting in 1992.'[5] If Patrick Kavanagh had seen it he might have written a poem about it.

Foxes approach houses not just in the city but also in the country. Every evening a fox comes to the lawn of Ballinahinch Castle Hotel for food. 'We started feeding him two years ago, and he will now take food from our hands. He seems totally fearless and pays no heed to people photographing him. At present he is resplendent in his winter coat.'[6]

'We are quite used to seeing fox cubs playing in our garden. In spring 1994, one which was tamer than the others used to come and take food which I had laid out, and eventually took it gently from my hand. One day I watched her tossing a piece of stick, so I did the same. At first she drew back, but then saw that I was joining in, and we played around the lawn. She took a few things, a sponge and two tools from the garage, and left them behind a wall. I called her Rusty and she continued to come for food every day until the end of November; she stopped then and didn't come when I called. I suppose she was growing up.'[7] Foxes are adult at about eight months, so this one probably went off to find a mate, a den and a territory.

'I am used to the barking of dog foxes and the heart-stopping mating calls of vixens in the early hours. But what is the high-pitched, whistling cry I hear from time to time; is it just more of the fox's repertoire?'[8] The fox expert, David McDonald, describes an interactive call between foxes at close quarters, which is like a high-pitched whine. The heart-stopping call is not confined to the vixen; he has seen dog foxes screaming on the move, 'pausing only for long enough to put their whole body into the effort of the call'. In earlier and more superstitious times these calls were attributed to the banshee and foreshadowed a death in the family that heard it.

Badgers make grunting or snuffling noises as they forage in the undergrowth. They live on earthworms, beetles, larvae, slugs, young rabbits, fruit, grass, roots, almost anything edible that is available. One correspondent found one munching away in her strawberry bed,[9] and, of course, they also love honey. 'In a rough, grassy area of my garden, some animal came and rooted out a bees' nest and scattered the honeycomb all over the place. What animal would do this?'[10] Badgers are also fond of wasps' nests, from which they eat the adults and the larvae. 'Every autumn after heavy rain some animal digs out the wasps' nests on our land. The nests are in low banks that border the laneway.'[11] It will also dig holes in the lawn, in searching for worms and grubs.

If badgers are proof against bee and wasp stings, they can also force a hedgehog to uncurl with their powerful front claws, and can' even bite through the coat of spines. Hedgehogs seem to know this and when they meet a badger will not roll up in their usually defensive position; instead they tuck their heads in and scream piteously. 'I was awakened by what I thought was a baby crying in the garden, and was more than surprised when my torch shone on a badger which was pinning a hedgehog under him. I hit the badger and he ran off without giving me a glance. The skin on the poor hedgehog's face was completely ripped off and it kept whimpering like a child. I put it on straw in a barrel and prayed for it to be healed. Two weeks later it was happy to say goodbye and scampered out of sight into the undergrowth.'[12]

Another reader had a more frontal encounter: 'Cycling a country by-road at 9.30 one evening, I came across a young badger examining a discarded can on the side of the road. Surprised, both of us stopped to watch the other with equal curiosity. As I walked closer to him he became alarmed and snorted loudly, a noise not unlike a cat spitting. I stopped immediately and at once he trotted towards me like a dog. Glancing at his sharp claws I retreated slightly, causing the badger to hiss and snort again. As his eyes seemed trained on my unprotected ankles, I decided discretion was the better part of valour and cycled on. What a pity I was not brave enough to stand my ground!'[13] There was no threat in the badger's behaviour, just wariness and curiosity; a young badger may not have had any reason to fear humans. What sounded like a hiss could well have been a noisy sniff, badgers rely as much on scent as on sight.

'The children and I noticed scratch marks in a few ash trees, up to a height of about three feet, which have removed the outermost bark layer at the back. Are they a badger's territorial marks?'[14] Badgers are social animals, living in small groups called 'clans', and they scent-mark and defend the boundary of their territory against other badgers. But when they scratch trees, usually one near the sett entrance, it is to stretch and sharpen their claws.

Badgers are generally nocturnal, and are only rarely seen abroad in daylight. But do they hibernate? A schoolboy asked the question to settle a difference of opinion with a teacher.[15] The answer is that Irish badgers do not hibernate in the strict biological sense, but they may be much less active in winter than in summer. In colder, more northern climates they stay in their setts and live on their stored fat. They sleep, but not as deeply as, say, the hedgehog, and can be roused more easily. Their heartbeat, breathing and metabolism do not decrease appreciably. Irish badgers may also sleep a lot in winter, but they come out of their setts regularly to feed, even in snowy and frosty weather.

Badgers have good reason to fear humans, who have always treated them abominably. Men set dogs on them in badger-baiting sessions; they have been infected with tuberculosis by cows, and farmers blame them for reinfecting their cattle and threaten them with extermination. In a more constructive approach, the Department of Agriculture has been carrying out long-term trials in west Cork, vaccinating the badgers orally by leaving out small, chocolate-coated cakes, laced with the vaccine, within the badgers' usual feeding territory.[16] If the project is successful, the future might be brighter for an inoffensive animal.

'We have a strange noise in the garden. It has moved about from one part to another, but it always comes from dense hedging or trees. The noise is a little like a muffled, choking, wheezy cough, not very loud. We have strained our eyes but cannot see anything.'[17] Top marks for hedgehog camouflage! A hedgehog in the garden is a great advantage as it feeds on slugs, and supplying some extra rations helps to keep them there; dog-food fits their diet more naturally than the traditional bread-and-milk.

Most hedgehog letters concern hibernation. 'During a fairly bright period in the early afternoon on Christmas Day, I was surprised to see a hedgehog rooting in the front garden. Are not hedgehogs nocturnal animals that usually hibernate during a cold mid-winter period?'[18] 'Out walking one evening in early October, I came across a wandering hedgehog in imminent danger of being run over. I gathered him up in my anorak and brought him home where he took up residence under the tool shed. We fed him unsalted peanuts and small amounts of dog food which he consumed nightly. We have not seen him since mid-November, is he hibernating?'[19]

He might foolishly have wandered out on a road again, because in Ireland and Britain hedgehogs do not usually hibernate until late-December or January. They remain active as long as there is food available to build up the fat reserves necessary to see them through hibernation. When the temperature drops they retire to winter quarters and become inactive, their blood temperature drops and their metabolism almost stops. Hibernation seems to be triggered by three factors: cold weather, scarcity of food and the amount of fat the hedgehog has accumulated. But some will awaken at times during the winter period and look for food, move to another nest, or even build a new one.

Humans with cars are the greatest enemy of the hedgehog, and one correspondent tells of a baby urchin probably orphaned by a road accident. 'While driving in my avenue gate I spotted a very small hedgehog about the size of an avocado pear. Its prickles were soft and I turned it over to see if it was damaged. There was no apparent damage but it let out a series of piercing peeps which continued after I put it safely down on the grass. I did not know that they "spoke", and I'm sure the mother could hear even if several hundred yards away.'[20] Such a small hedgehog would be unlikely to survive: it would not have learned to forage for itself, and would be very vulnerable to a predator.

The stoat, sometimes wrongly called a weasel in this country, is a member of the mustelid family, which includes the badger, mink, pine marten and otter: they all have musk-glands at the base of their tails. In more northern climates stoats turn white in winter and are the 'ermine' whose long, thin pelts adorned the cloaks of kings and merchants. In Ireland they retain their usual chestnut brown fur with a white belly-stripe all year round. The fearlessness of the stoat has particularly impressed correspondents: 'When we were building a hide in our tree house, my brother Edward spotted what he thought was a mink. When I looked it was gone and I said it was probably a rat. Just then a cheeky stoat popped out from under the hedge. It pranced up to us to get a good look. I frightened him away with a branch but he came back six times. He then climbed up a stone wall and halfway up a tree before jumping off and running away.'[21]

'I watched a stoat dragging a dead rabbit across a building site while being menaced by a procession of noisy rooks and jackdaws. The stoat pulled the rabbit under a builders' sign at the end of the road and disappeared, Two hours later I saw what I presumed to be the same stoat repeat the process, but this time he then emerged from under the board, went to a pool of water and took a long drink, totally oblivious of the human audience. He returned to the second rabbit, re-emerged and dragged it a further twenty-five yards before disappearing into the undergrowth. Are these creatures so voracious that they and their young can consume two rabbits in such a short time?'[22] A stoat eats about a third of its own weight every day and as the number of kits in a litter may be as high as nine or ten, and both parents bring food to the den, they could easily manage two rabbits, which are an important part of stoat diet.

Indeed, the stoat is often seen wrapped around a rabbit's neck and biting into it. 'I observed a young rabbit being attacked by a stoat while other rabbits ran around in a panic. An adult rabbit charged the stoat and drove it away, but the young rabbit later died. About ten minutes later the stoat returned and hauled it away.'[23] Another correspondent saw the classic distraction tactic of the stoat: 'Near Mullaghmore in Co Sligo, we came on a small warren where the rabbits were alert and restless. Then we saw a stoat making short leaps and runs around the perimeter, and it continued this ballet-like performance for a time.'[24] The dancing of stoats to mesmerise their prey, birds as well as rabbits, is regular behaviour.

Many readers were surprised that stoats swim, and even more so that they fish: the phenomenon generated a lively correspondence. One observer, walking along a Sligo shore 'noticed a stoat emerge from some loose rock several yards above the high water mark. It was low tide at the time and the stoat made its way down to the water's edge, disappearing behind a ledge, in a few seconds it reappeared carrying in its mouth a small, live rock-fish.'[25]

This brought another letter, from the Co Clare naturalist John MacNamara, telling a slightly different story. 'Here on the Burren coastline the ebb tide leaves many rock pools, with clear water often no deeper than eight or nine inches and no vegetation or stones to hide the little fish. The boss stoat comes on his rounds, peruses the fish but dare not go in. He gyrates around the pool as if electrified, frightening the little fish who sees this predator and has nowhere to hide. The fish circles dementedly until he runs out of oxygen and consequently dies after a few minutes, floating to the top of the pool in the process. The marauding stoat just picks him up from the water and scoots back to his base. They like the little fish very much when rearing the young.'[26]

The letter drew another in support, remarking that the tactic was similar to that employed by the stoat to mesmerise a rabbit, but claiming that the fish was not dead but winded. He then went on to describe a similar tactic used by young men chasing pike on Annagh Lake, near Ballyhaunis when it freezes over quickly with thick, transparent ice. They 'drive nails in the soles of their boots with the points exposed downwards, and run across the lake in search of pike, which can be found up to nearly five pounds weight. When one is located, they run it hard until it turns on its back motionless after, perhaps, three hundred yards. The hunters then knock a small hole in the ice with a hammer and extract their trophy. This must be done speedily because the fish otherwise recovers inside a minute or two and departs unimpaired.'[27]

Another mustelid is enjoying a recovery in numbers on this island. 'Recently we caught a pine marten here in Tipperary. Years ago, in Co Waterford, we had to give up keeping sheep as they were, allegedly, being killed by a pine marten. We were told that it had a hard spike on its tail which bored into the sheep and killed it. There was no evidence of this spike on the animal we caught, so we wonder if it is just an Old Wives' Tale.'[28] More like an Old Bachelors' Tale; they're even sillier. The pine marten will certainly feed on dead sheep which is why it was decimated by strychnine-laced carcasses put out by farmers to kill foxes and marauding dogs. There is no evidence that the pine marten's diet runs to live things bigger than a rabbit.

This shy and beautiful creature was virtually wiped out in Ireland, but is now a protected species and making a remarkable comeback in recent years. Its stronghold is Co Clare where it has given satisfaction to one reader. 'At last there is something to control the grey crow and magpie rampage. Pine martens are shinning up trees and bushes and robbing their nests, which has brought them back to acceptable proportions here in west Clare. Obviously this won't apply in open country, but in enclosed country they are extremely effective. Unfortunately it does not augur well for kestrels, merlins and sparrowhawks, as their droppings on the ground and screaming for food will give their locations away to the marten.'[29] Moreover, when the pine marten cleans out the nest it may use it as a den, curling up to sleep in the gently-swaying branches,

Eye on Nature had reports of martens from Counties Mayo, Clare, Cork, Galway, Leitrim and Tipperary, and some letters suggest that it is not as shy as we might have thought. As a Co Leitrim correspondent came out the front door of his house one night, he saw a pine marten in his damson tree. 'Its head was about four inches high, with small, round-topped ears. It was a brown colour with white under the chin and belly. It wasn't a cat.'[30] The Irish name for the pine marten is *cat crainn* or tree-cat, and although it lives mainly on birds or animals, it eats fruit and nuts, earthworms and insects; indeed, a non-stop Roman feast of casual morsels.

A Co Clare pine marten was even more precocious. 'In October my brother and I heard a commotion in the utility room and found our Jack Russell barking furiously at something under the freezer. We got the dog away and waited for the intruder to come out, a pine marten! Some time later my mother was putting clothes in the washing machine when she discovered its droppings in the drum. We have sighted the pine marten several times since then, as it is a regular visitor to our dust bin.'[31]

Since their introduction into Ireland for breeding on fur farms in 1951, and a first sighting in the wild in Co Tyrone a decade later, the American mink has taken out irrevocable Irish citizenship. It is now established along the waterways of every county, and when young animals are dispersing in late summer, after the breeding season, they catch the human eye in new places. 'We have observed black mink at the mouth of the Ballinglen River which flows through Ballycastle, Co Mayo, into Bunatrahir Bay. One evening, we watched one swimming in the river before heading for some nearby rabbit warrens. The animal seemed confident and unafraid. Presumably, having no natural enemies, it will thrive in Mayo to the detriment of other species.'[32] It is characteristic of the mink that it is not afraid of humans, and it is now part of Ireland's wildlife community. Chris Smal, who has studied mink for the Wildlife Service, accepts that it is here to stay. With some local loss in the duck and water-bird populations, it will eventually space itself out alongside the country's native predators.

A Co Wicklow correspondent is not so sanguine. 'We are suffering from an invasion of mink, often sighted but never caught. Our once numerous moorhens have virtually vanished, and the mallards no longer breed on the pond. Last week, my son found a moorhen tangled in discarded fishing line and hooks; while freeing it he saw a mink creeping towards him looking for a free dinner! But by far the most serious incident was the killing of a neighbour's entire flock of laying hens. We have tried baited mink traps with no success, and obviously poison is out of the question.'[33]

All small mustelids, and foxes too, will indulge in surplus killing when the prey is confined, in a hen-house, for example. The birds are unable to escape as they would in the wild, and the predator gets over-stimulated and kills all of them. Sometimes domestic birds die of fright and that accounts for the absence of marks on some of them. If we pen birds, we should make sure that their stockades are predator-proof.

'While on holidays in west Cork our two boys saw a swift, black creature making its way up a steep sandy bank from the sea. We thought it was too thin, small and black to be an otter and decided it was a mink. But a few days later the boys spotted it, or a close relative, swimming in the sea quite far from the shore. We have never heard of a mink swimming in salt water.'[34] Mink do swim in the sea, and will travel up to three kilometres between islands.

In the early expansion of feral mink, there were fears that they might reduce our native otters by competing for waterway territories. This seems, in fact, not to have happened, least of all along our coasts. We do not have the 'sea otter', a quite different species confined to America's Pacific coast, but just the ordinary European otter, which is as happy fishing in the sea as in lakes and rivers. 'On the Iveragh Peninsula I watched an otter cub gambolling on the shore, while an adult otter slipped smoothly into the water, scarcely disturbing the silent inlet. Later we watched the adult being mobbed by a pair of herring gulls when it resurfaced. It received the same attention from a great black-backed gull which repeatedly hung in the air above the otter's course, dropping like a stone towards its head as it surfaced. I assume it had caught something and the gull was attempting piracy.'[35]

Otters are common residents all along the west coast, where they often make their holts, or dens, in peat-banks and dunes. 'In early March, while sitting alone on some rocks sheltering from the rain and hail, on a beach near Louisburgh in Co Mayo, I got a very special thrill. An otter came out of the sea and zigzagged over the rocks quite close to where I was sitting. He climbed up one of the sand dunes and disappeared into a hole. In my excitement I forgot about the hail that was beating on my face and waited to see if he would reappear. But the otter had more cop-on, he stayed in out of the foul weather. I pulled the hood of my anorak tighter and went back to where I came from.'[36] It would have been a long wait, because the otter had had a meal and would lie up for many hours in the daytime burrow.

'On Mannin beach during the Christmas holiday we met an otter. It stood still on the sand until one of my children became a little excited, and then ran to a rock pool where it took shelter for a while. We followed to get a better look, as it was the first time we had seen an otter in the wild. It then crossed a small strand and hid under an overhanging rock, where it curled up and rested. We then left it alone. The otter's nose was very pink, almost raw looking, could it have been exhausted after a fight?'[37]

An otter will sometimes get a scarred nose from an argument with a crab, but this animal's behaviour suggests that it could have been sick. In the late 1980s there was some concern that the 'distemper' virus which had been killing the common seal might also begin to infect our coastal otters, but that did not seem to happen. Coincidentally, we also encountered a sick otter on our strand at around the same time.

Eye on Nature has once or twice had a phone call asking what one should do with an orphaned otter cub. Several naturalist authors have written delightful accounts of their rescue activities.[38] First, it seems, make sure that the cub is abandoned and not just waiting for its mother's return. The young otter needs four-hourly feeds of milk (diluted goat's milk, not cow's milk which it would find indigestible), with the addition of egg yolk as a substitute for colostrom for a very young cub and also some cod liver oil. It needs its bottom wiped after feeding to stimulate it to defecate. After about a month the period between feeds gets longer, and at seven weeks the cub needs fish as well; milk is discontinued at fourteen weeks. Before that, the cub should be introduced to a river so that it can learn to swim.

After the mink, another exotic and feral member of the mustelid family made an appearance in Monaghan in the late 1980s, but it has not achieved the same success in the wild. 'Around 1987 I hit and killed an animal with a description similar to that of the pine marten. When I went back to see what I had killed, it had been joined by two three-quarter-sized animals of the same species. They were quite unafraid and only ran away when I was within feet of them. The corpse had a very strong smell. The coat had long, dark-brown hair, but the shorter hair on the underside was cream. I telephoned the local wildlife ranger who came and identified it as a polecat ferret that had gone feral and said that it was the first reported case of them breeding in the wild. The large size was explained by an abundant food supply.'[39] Polecats are making a return in the wild in some parts of Britain; crossed with ferrets, they are known as polecat ferrets. They are domesticated and used as hunters in both Britain and Northern Ireland.

The only herd of native red deer in Ireland is at Killarney, which has also supplied the stock for reintroduction in the Connemara National Park. Elsewhere, red deer have been introduced from Scotland. The native species has been joined by two others: fallow and sika deer. Fallow deer were originally introduced into Ireland by the Normans, and more were later brought in to private parks and escaped into the wild. They are found in all of the four provinces, in habitats which mix woodland and open pasture. Sika deer were first imported from Japan by Lord Powerscourt in 1861, and they too escaped, hybridising with red deer in Wicklow and sharing the range of the red deer at Killarney. The Wicklow hybrids can be puzzling: 'In mid-July, at the forestry east of the Vartry plateau in Co Wicklow I saw some strange deer, a hind with two fawns, obviously this year's, and a large stag in velvet, four points to the antlers. Another hind joined him but saw me and crashed away. The others followed out on the open hill. I have never seen twins before, nor the stag in a family group. In all aspects they were sika, except for their colour which was very dark, almost black, the colour of a very dark, chestnut pony, and only a faint trace of white on the rump of the hind.'[40] The second fawn may have belonged to the second hind; and the stag may have been rounding up his harem, somewhat early, perhaps, in preparation for the rutting season.

All three species of deer are found in Co Wicklow, and the following correspondent did not say which one he saw. 'While walking in the

Glenmalure area, suddenly from the forest path I saw an almost fully-grown deer being chased by a large fox. On seeing men, the fox was distracted and the deer escaped. I never knew that foxes preyed on deer, but further evidence lay on the path a short distance on, the carcase of a fully grown deer, stripped to the bone with just the head and hooves remaining. Is it possible that the fox is now evolving into the gap left by the wolf?'[41] The scene bears another interpretation: that poachers were at work, that the fox had been drawn by the gift of carrion, and that both deer and fox were fleeing some further disturbance.

Anyone who has witnessed the rabbit's mad dash for the burrow when a human or a dog enters a warren will be surprised by the following letter: 'As I was walking along a deep drain with my spaniel I spied a rabbit travelling along the opposite bank. I shortly came to a T-junction of drains and saw something swimming towards me across about fifteen yards of open water. It proved to be the rabbit which swam strongly towards me and the dog, clambered out, shook itself and passed within a few yards of us. It was neither chased nor frightened and seemed oblivious of us.'[42]

Some rabbits are black, and this black fur is a genetic aberration, like albinism, and occurs throughout the population. 'Recently while walking in the grounds of a nearby school, I saw a number of rabbits near a hedge and one of them was black.'[43] This phenomenon is more usually found among island populations, where there are fewer ground predators and a badly camouflaged animal has a better chance of survival and of passing on the gene.

What do you do about a baby rabbit in danger? 'Recently we saved a baby rabbit from the clutches of a hawk. It was badly wounded but we brought it back to health. It is feeding now, should we put it back in the field where we found it?'[44] There was an old belief that if you saved a person's life, you were responsible for it afterwards. So, too, with baby rabbits. Having been forced to abandon its home, it would not survive without one of its own. It might have been better to leave the predator to its prey: should the mouse be rescued from the cat, or the snail from the thrush?

The old, pre-decimal, Irish currency sported a hare on the *leith-real* or threepenny bit, but it was a brown hare, not the Irish hare. The native Irish hare is a subspecies of the Arctic hare, very different from the brown hare of the rest of Europe. 'In mid-March, when driving from Hollywood up towards the Wicklow Gap, I saw an animal running across the road which I took to be a brown-and-white terrier. At closer range it turned out to be a hare with the upper part of the body mainly brown and the underparts mainly white. I believe hares can become white in cold climes. Do they do this in elevated areas of Ireland and was this hare in the process of changing?'[45] In winter the Irish hare turns rarely, if ever, fully white; and in summer it turns brown again, except for the tail.

NOTES

NINE

THE MOUSE THAT ATE WINKLES

Red squirrels are native to Ireland, but for the last four centuries they have had an uncertain, even endangered, existence. Up to the eighteenth century they were hunted for food and for their pelts. They also ran into habitat problems and became almost extinct in both Ireland and Britain: because of the break-up of the forests into smaller units, they couldn't travel from one area to another when food was scarce.

Red squirrels were reintroduced into this country in the nineteenth century, but some observers think it likely that they hadn't died out completely but 'survived in a pocket where forest or wood cover allowed'.[1] Grey squirrels were introduced into Co Longford in 1911 and have spread widely since then. The predominant theme of *Eye on Nature* letters about squirrels has been the charge that they drive out their red, more desirable, cousins. But another school of thought holds that grey squirrels don't actually drive the red variety out, but replace them when they suffer local extinction.

Views have been strongly held. 'I'm afraid I can't agree that grey squirrels don't drive out the red one but merely replace them when they die out, Since the arrival of the grey squirrels in this area eighteen months ago, the red squirrels, both in Mount Juliet and in my new farm at Norelands, have completely disappeared. The woods are swarming with the greys. They have driven out or killed all the reds. They have also sadly diminished most of the small bird life. They are, of course, tree rats and should be treated as vermin, not as cuddly pets. Like the mink they should never have been introduced to this country. I miss the red squirrels: I know of at least three pairs in my woods.'[2]

'Round here, mid-way between Baltinglass and Dunlavin in Co

Wicklow, has always been a stronghold of the red squirrel, but I saw my very first grey some five to ten years ago. Now they are almost as common as the reds, and they are to be seen in the same woods. Inevitably, I suppose, the reds will be reduced in numbers.'[3]

Recent research in Britain on the effect of grey squirrels on the red population makes the following points: (a) grey squirrels are no more aggressive to red squirrels than to their own kind; (b) red squirrels are adapted for conifer forests and greys for deciduous, so greys have an advantage in mixed forests: grey squirrels eat acorns, while red squirrels cannot because of their tannin content; (c) hazel nuts, a staple of the red population, have got scarcer because coppices are not as widespread as in the past; and grey squirrels can eat hazel nuts before they are ripe and therefore clear them before the reds get their opportunity; (d) the one area where greys are likely to be a direct threat to the reds is medical: biologists have found a virus which was killing off red squirrels but not affecting greys; furthermore it only occurred where the two populations mixed, so it seems likely that grey squirrels introduced the virus while retaining an immunity to it.

Red squirrels have been making something of a comeback, probably due to the increase in conifer forestry, and there have been sightings in many areas where they had disappeared. 'Our red squirrels, having been absent for some months, have returned. We have very few acorns and hazelnuts this year, 1991, and they are looking for food to bury for the winter. Should I put hazelnuts in the trees or on the ground? They live mostly in the woods which, alas, are now hunted by semi-wild cats.'[4] As the squirrels have moved back they must have decided that there is enough food for them for the winter; the feral cats, of course pose a new threat to them.

The rest of the Irish rodents are not among the favourite animals of humans, but one correspondent gave another, refreshing point of view: 'I am curious to know how many kinds of rats there are in Ireland. I found a most attractive specimen taking nuts from the bird feeder. It was a sort of reddish-grey, very shiny and clean with big, bright eyes and dainty, pink feet. He'd take a nut or two and scamper off to some nest or other in the opposite bank, then scamper back, up a branch and take more nuts. I was quite taken with the little creature as there was nothing creepy or sinister about him, rather the opposite.'[5]

Since it ousted the black rat two hundred and fifty years ago, the brown rat, *Rattus norvegicus*, is the standard Irish rat of town and country. We watched one on our bird table recently and it was quite a handsome animal, but many people do not like its hairless tail. Freshly groomed and on a fine day it can look unexpectedly appealing. These moments are good for us if only to remind us of our burden of prejudices and phobic fears.

The antics of mice, however, provide interest and amusement for many readers. A Co Waterford reader had a most extraordinary experience. 'Something strange has been happening in my kitchen. Before retiring I make up a bird pudding so that I can feed my feathered friends early in the morning. I leave it on top of the freezer in a shallow dish with a small, plastic bowl loosely covering it. Also on the freezer are a few pots of herbs and geranium cuttings. The other morning I was surprised to see that the parsley had been stripped to bare stalks and some of the scented geranium leaves had also disappeared, On removing the cover of the pudding there were all the missing leaves beautifully placed on top of the food.

'The following night it came again, not only purloining more parsley leaves but digging into the geranium cutting pot, distributing compost everywhere and piling some on top of the pudding. It had the look of something making a nest. My son suggested putting flour around the area to show up footprints. Next morning, with fresh compost now completely surrounding the bowl, there were clear markings of little feet or teeth.

'My husband was banned from setting a trap: we wanted to see more. The digging went on for several more nights with me refilling the pot each day until my housewifely streak took over and I cleared the whole freezer top.

'But the mystery continued, this time on the kitchen top near the sink. The birds' scraps were covered again, this time with fragments of egg shell, a Brillo pad and bristles neatly chewed from my pastry brush, the whole mixture covered with small pieces of kitchen foil from under the hot plate of the cooker. This morning it was the Spontex pad in myriad blue pieces.

'My husband, down first in the morning, has twice surprised what he took to be a mouse scurrying away from the scene of the crime. Might it be a shrew? We are both loth to harm whatever it is that works so diligently and is such an opportunist.'[6]

It was, indeed, the ordinary house mouse, which is the only member of the mouse family that will build a nest in food; a mouse might spend her whole life in a sack of flour. She also uses whatever material is at hand to line the nest.

Then there was a shaggy mouse story: 'Our cat brought a mouse into the house one evening. Puss sat quietly while the mouse stroked one of the cat's paws. Anyone I told laughed hugely at me until a week later our son witnessed the same performance. Do cats and mice form pre-prandial relationships?'[7] In the peaceable kingdom 'the wolf shall dwell with the lamb and the leopard lie down with the kid' but there is no mention of the mouse stroking the cat!

'I have a strawberry bed covered with net which is weighed down at one side with a six-foot long piece of guttering. I noticed no berries ripening and the crop diminishing, and when I lifted the piece of guttering I found it packed at both ends, almost to the centre, with both ripe and unripe berries. What could have done this? No bird could get in and there are no squirrels around.'[8] That was the field mouse. *Apodemus sylvaticus* is slightly larger than the house mouse and also handsomer; it has a shiny, warm brown fur with black and yellow markings along the sides, a white chest and belly with a yellow-brown spot or stripe at the throat. And it is a hoarder.

Another reader sent in evidence of field mouse foraging. 'Enclosed are the stones of a wild cherry which have been eaten into for the kernels by a very small animal. The teeth marks are clearly visible. Note how evenly the holes are made and always across the split lines. Is this a harvest, wood or field mouse? I have found caches of these all around the garden.'[9] The harvest mouse is not found in Ireland, and wood mouse is another name for the field mouse, the name commonly used in this country. The cherry stones were eaten by a field mouse. There is an identical picture of a cherry stone in *Collins Guide to Animal Tracks and Signs* .

Apodemus is also an opportunistic feeder. 'I was on the shore near Bangor harbour with my Dad, and just below us were some rocks covered with seaweed uncovered by the falling tide. I noticed movement among the seaweed and saw what appeared to be several mice moving around. One of them picked up a small shell like a winkle, got the contents out and ate it.'[10] This behaviour was entirely new to us, but the field mouse will eat a snail, so why not a seafood cocktail?

The sighting of an alien mouse was recorded in one letter: 'My wife and I were walking along the south-facing banks at Sutton when we saw a medium-sized rodent with clear white markings on both sides of its snout. They were rectangular and ran from its eyes to its nose. I have failed to find any reference to this creature in any book on Irish fauna.'[11] This fits the description of the edible dormouse which must have been introduced or is an escaped pet. The Romans used to fatten them for the table, hence the name. They were introduced into Britain about a century ago, but not into Ireland except as pets.

'I once saw a strange little creature on Bull Island. As it scurried across our path I thought it was a large bumble bee, but on closer look the tiny creature seemed to be made up of a brown fuzzy body and a longish, thin tail. I wondered was it a shrew?'[12] It was a pygmy shrew, our smallest mammal, and the only shrew found in Ireland. It is not a rodent, although it bears superficial resemblance to a mouse, and its teeth are all tipped with red.

Because they are so small, pygmy shrews must eat one-and-a- half times their own weight each day to maintain their body heat and stay alive, so they spend almost all their time foraging. 'On a holiday in Kerry, we stayed in a disused farmhouse near Portmagee. We shared it with two pygmy shrews who pattered all over the floor at any hour of day or night. They moved like two clockwork toys, in abrupt, random directions, chasing beetles or woodlice. We could converse quite normally while they ran about underfoot. We put out a small cube of cooked meat, but the shrews found it so large that one had to get up on his hind legs to attack it. Eventually it was taken off into a hole in the wall.'[13]

This is a very interesting observation because research has shown the pygmy shrew to be very aggressive to other shrews except in the breeding season which lasts from April to August. Perhaps they were a mating pair. Pygmy shrews live for less than a year-and-a-half. Those that are born in summer, if they survive the winter, breed the following summer and die before winter to be replaced by the new young.

There are nine species of bat in Ireland, two different varieties of pipistrelles are just newly discovered and all are insect feeders. Because of their nocturnal habits, very few of the general public can tell them apart; they see them darting about at dusk and in the early morning, or hear them moving about or squeaking in their attics. Bats can also be heard squeaking in flight, but these audible sounds are not the echo-location transmissions which they use for hunting: they are communications with other bats and are territorial, recognition or warning calls. Their hunting transmissions are ultra-sonic.

Some correspondents are concerned when they find bats in their attics. 'I have seventy-five to one hundred bats in my attic. They've increased in the last few years. How should I get rid of them?'[14] 'We bought a house about a year ago and immediately discovered bats in one attic, but this did not cause a problem. However, we have installed an attic stairs, and are now reluctant to store anything there as the place is littered with droppings. We need the storage space and would like to provide alternative accommodation for the bats without harming them. Could we build something and place it in our large open sheds?'[15]

Bats are a protected species and if they are all-year-round residents in the attic they are best dealt with by experts.[16] There are several different bats that roost in the roof space of houses, among other types of buildings. Some, like the whiskered bat, the brown long-eared bat and Natterer's bat, use the location as a maternity roost, and in autumn they leave the attic to hibernate during the winter in the cooler ambience of caves or mines, cellars or tunnels. However, Leisler's bat and the serotine might well stay put for the winter. The serotine can be identified by its bullet-shaped droppings which collect beneath the roosting site, but colonies can be quite small as bat colonies go, ranging from ten to fifty and only exceptionally up to one hundred.

Pipistrelles, the most familiar of our bats, are tiny, a mere 40mm long, and they often use the eaves of houses, the spaces behind fascia board, or other crevices, as maternity colonies. But one correspondent found some in a very peculiar roost. 'In early July, when I was looking at bathroom fixtures in a showroom of the warehouse type, I saw what looked like black, charred paper in the plug holes of several baths. In fact they were groups of bats with their noses pointing down into the hole and their legs outwards. The assistant had declared war on them and threatened to seal up all the entrance holes. I thought that bats hung upside down from ceilings by their feet.'[17]

The lesser horseshoe bat and Daubenton's bat rarely come to modern houses and prefer large, old buildings; they hibernate under bridges, in old castles and tunnels or caves. Daubenton's bat is the one that is seen skimming over water. They pick insects out of the air or off the water, using their large feet. 'I was fishing a floating fly on a small lake in Mayo when very much to my surprise I hooked a bat by the tail. Holding the torch in my mouth I gently unhooked it, but it was quite exhausted. I placed it on my fishing bag and after about ten minutes it shook itself and flew away. I am told by other anglers that it is not uncommon for a bat to take an artificial fly in the air, but I had no idea that they took flies, artificial or otherwise, off the surface of the water.'[18] Another reader had a similar experience: 'I was fishing one night on a Connemara river with a Hugh Falkus surface lure, which is a piece of cork one-and-a-half inches by three-quarters of an inch with a hook whipped to it, when it was taken by a bat.'[19] These were both Daubenton's bats which emerge quite late in the evening when it is fully dark, and so are not so well known to those of us that do not frequent waterways at night.

There were several reports of bats flying during the day. 'Late in March in the early afternoon, I was walking outside Athboy, Co Meath when I noticed what I first thought was a bird with an unusual form of flight. Then I realised it was a bat with the usual swerving, fluttering pattern about ten to fifteen feet above the road. After a few minutes it disappeared into a laurel hedge and did not re-emerge.'[20] And from Co Mayo: 'On the same day that your Co Meath reader saw a bat flying in the middle of the day, I saw a long-eared bat in a garden here in Castlebar. At first I thought it was an injured bird, because it flew a couple of inches and then flew again. My neighbour, who is a pilot, explained that the bat's echolocation system does not function well during the day'[21] and 'Our local school has a colony of bats living happily in the roof. In October the school children saw them flying in and out at lunchtime and they would like to know why.'[22]

Although bats hibernate when the cold weather arrives in October, they will emerge to feed even in daylight during mild spells. They also fly in daylight in spring when they emerge from hibernation and are hungry. In the cooler weather of spring and autumn there are not so many insects flying at night, so they are forced to feed during the day. Bats avoid flying during the day, not because of their echolocation system which is sonar rather than radar, but because it is much more dangerous as they are clearly visible to predators. A survey in Britain found that a bat was one thousand times more at risk of being eaten by hawks during day flight.

Another reason is that they run the risk of overheating, as the sun strikes the bare skin of their wings.

'In previous years there have been occasional sightings of bats on the stretch of road near our house. In mid-November, however, there was a dramatic increase in numbers which a big increase in moths might account for. The only street light for a mile or so is outside the house, and it attracts moths of all sizes. Beneath it was a veritable shooting gallery as the bats closed in like guided missiles with radar locked on targets. The kids preferred the spectacle to television. How far do bats travel to feed?'[23] Bats will travel a kilometre or more to a feeding area, and they remain loyal to a territory. Mid-November was late for both moths and bats to be airborne so the weather must have been very mild.

Although cats and dogs are not strictly wildlife they are as much a part of nature as we are. Cats get themselves involved in many back garden dramas but few as bizarre as this: 'While sitting in the garden yesterday I heard a commotion from the dense rhododendron bushes five yards to my right. This lasted for about ten seconds or so when out flew what I thought were two huge pigeons, one in hot pursuit of the other. The leading one quickly lost height and thudded, with a sickeningly loud thump, into a tall, ground-floor window, about ten yards away to my left.

'To my surprise a sparrowhawk and my small, grey-white, inveterate hunter of a cat, dropped to the ground. The bird was much more stunned than the cat. I dropped a blanket on it and went for my bird identification book. It was slate-grey on top, yellow beak, legs and eyes, and larger than a large pigeon. The hawk recovered in about half-an-hour and was let free. Did the cat spring on to the bird and make it lose height? Did the bird grab, then drop, the cat? There were two marks on the window, the higher one covered with feathers.'[24]

This is our reconstruction: The description makes it a male sparrowhawk, which is much smaller than the female and thus not as strong; it preys on smaller birds than the hen which can easily take wood pigeons. A search of the rhododendrons might have found the blackbird, for example, which the hawk had pursued into the bushes. This was July and the male does the hunting in the breeding season. He usually plucks the prey and tears off the head for himself, before taking it home to his mate and the chicks. We suspect that the hawk was busy at this work when he was jumped by the cat, which then hung on for the most surprising journey of its life.

Since the influx of foxes into urban areas, cat owners worry for the safety of their pets, and there were several letters seeking reassurance. 'There is a fox which we have seen quite regularly at dusk crossing over the cultivated part of our garden. Would he have any interest in our cat?'[25] 'My cat, Amigo, chases foxes and appears to make a game out of it, doing a dance, stopping, then away again until he chases the fox out of his territory. There appears to me to be a different relationship between cats and foxes than that between cats and dogs. Amigo is terrified of dogs and will take off like a bat out of hell as soon as he sees one,'[26] It probably depends on whose territory is being invaded.

'I was chatting to a neighbour at the top of one of my fields when I heard a commotion on the other side of the hedge. To my great surprise I saw our cat running at full stretch, with a large fox in close pursuit. It took refuge in a nearby tree and the fox ambled away towards a copse where I believe there is a den. I had understood, from evidence such as the BBC documentary on the urban foxes of Bristol, that, in the wild, foxes and cats ignore each other. Was this fox, perhaps, intent on seeing off a cat which disturbed its den in the breeding season?'[27] In urban settings, foxes and cats meet more frequently and sometimes eat side-by-side. This cat, may, indeed, have shown too much curiosity about the mewings of suckling fox cubs.

How sensitive are animals to atmospheric changes? This letter came from Brussels in 1992: 'At 3.00am one morning in April, I was woken by our cat making a strange, distressed, wailing sound. She was roundly scolded for spoiling my night's sleep. Precisely nineteen minutes later, as I was beginning to doze back to sleep again, the world began to move all around me. Our earthquake!'[28] And this one from a dog owner: 'The night of November 17th was one of broken sleep for my springer spaniel and for me. He barked, groaned, ran up and down stairs, and generally made a nuisance of himself. At one stage I wondered could there be anything astronomical afoot, especially as the sun's cycle is approaching maximum, and animals are more sensitive to certain phenomena than humans. Next day I read in *The Irish Times* that a display of the aurora borealis had indeed been seen in parts of the country. Could this have been the cause of my dog's unhappy night?'[29]

The early shock waves of an earthquake or the magnetic disturbance of the aurora might well be felt by animals before humans become conscious of them.   The seismic waves of an earthquake can be registered by instrumentation before we experience them.   The aurora borealis is caused by solar winds which generate electricity in space.   Billions of watts of electrical energy flow down the Earth's magnetic field towards the poles, where the atoms of the air are made to glow, like neon in a tube, in a coloured lighting display.   At the maximum of the sun's cycle, there are bright and frequent auroral displays on Earth.   Such magnetic disturbances can certainly disrupt the navigation of migrating bird: who knows what they do to dogs?

It surprised some readers to learn that dogs liked fruit, but there was plenty of evidence that they did.   One letter summed it up: 'Our boxer, Rosie, loves blackberries and is cute enough to eat only the ripe ones.   She also eats strawberries and raspberries straight from the plants, and has a passion for grapes which the children feed her when they think we're not looking.   Her most annoying habit is that of standing up on her hind legs against the apple and plum trees and reaching as high as she can for the fruit.'[30]   Our own dog, Meg, was also a fruit eater, and she loved garden peas and cabbage stalk.   The diet of foxes and wolves in the wild contains both fruit and vegetables and "carnivore" is a word we may throw around too lightly.

TEN

SPRINTING WITH DOLPHINS

A fresh awareness of the sea and its life is part of the new environmental sensibility we now enjoy. For an island people, an interest in dolphins, whales, seals and turtles is part of a wider reaching-out towards our maritime horizons.

Of our seals, the neat round head of the common or harbour seal is most often spotted by casual observers; the dog-like profile of the much larger grey seal belongs more typically to our Atlantic shores. Dublin Bay has a good population of harbour seals, and the special pleasure of glimpsing one in Dun Laoghaire harbour was caught by Laura, Amanda and Fiona in an early letter to *Eye on Nature*. 'It was lovely to see a wild seal so close to the busy pier with hundreds of people walking up and down.'[1] A Northside correspondent was equally appreciative. 'The seals were back on their sandbank on the south-eastern tip of Bull Island on October 9th. Through the field glasses I counted nine, and I could see one moving. Quite a sight to have from your bedroom window at low tide.'[2]

Dublin Bay also has a constant population of harbour porpoises. 'In late September, I was delighted to see a porpoise in the area of the Bailey lighthouse about one hundred metres offshore and five hundred metres on the Dublin city side. I had a clear view of it rising and dipping in the water directly below me on the cliff walk, and I could see and hear it blowing spray. It swam away towards Dun Laoghaire, and for a while I could see its back shining with the reflection of the sun.'[3] In a regular watch from Howth Head kept in 1994, anything from one to six were seen every ninety minutes in June, July and August. This dropped to one sighting every five hours from September to December; at that time of year it requires no little patience to see them.

The porpoises' big cousin, the dolphin, especially the bottle-nosed variety, demands and gains more attention since Fungie, the Dingle dolphin, took up with humans. 'On June 12th, with our friends the Turpins and their sailboard, we went on a family outing to the Silver Strand near the entrance to Killary Harbour. During the afternoon two schools of dolphins appeared, and one group of about ten was swimming within one hundred yards of the beach. Donal Turpin paddled the sail board, without its mast, out among them and found them immediately inquisitive and friendly. They circled around the sail board, diving under it in pairs and arching out of the water to breathe. He came into the beach and took the girls out to meet them, and then Juli and Rona paddled out to them on their own. The dolphins stayed playing around us for almost half-an-hour. It was the first time I had ever seen them, a wonderful thrill. But of course we'd forgotten the camera!'[4]

That same pod also accompanies the ferry from Cleggan to Inishbofin[5] and provided adventure further north along the coast for a Dublin visitor. 'I had snorkelled the length of Carramore Beach from the mouth of the river to Cuaneen Harbour, and with the weight of equipment, I was cold and tired and decided to walk back to the car. When I spotted a group of dolphins some distance out from the river mouth, I waded back into the water to waist level and slapped the surface with my fins. This attracted their attention, so with some apprehension, I donned my fins and mask again and swam out towards them. I was immediately surrounded by a dozen smiling faces which began an excited chatter with their high-pitched calls. The sound engulfed me with incredible volume. After a couple of minutes the sound subsided and, as if in turn, each dolphin approached me for a closer view. They would lie side on and roll their body so that one eye would look straight into my mask.

'For the next twenty minutes I enjoyed the thrill of a lifetime as these wild, bottle-nosed dolphins cavorted around me. As I sprinted on the surface they would zigzag below me in squadrons of two and three, all swimming in perfect formation. Often one or two dolphins would lie motionless in mid-water a few metres ahead, as if inviting me to chase. As I dived and reached out to touch them, they would take off at full steam, throwing up clouds of sand as their tails swept down on the seabed. This would immediately give rise to another outburst of excited conversation among them.

'Unlike the Dingle dolphin, Fungie, whom I have visited on two occasions, these dolphins would not allow me to touch them. Moreover they appeared to be just as excited to be playing tag with this strange swimmer as I was with them. With all the sprinting and diving I eventually tired and reluctantly bade farewell to these wonderful creatures. I will always remember that evening off Carramore Beach as the most privileged and magical of my diving career.'[6]

Fungie has made people more conscious of dolphins. 'On a Wayfarer weekend to observe the flowers and birds of the Burren, we were delighted to witness a large group of dolphins, leaping high out of the water, singly and in twos and threes. The spectacular display continued for a considerable time, rendered more beautiful by the colours of the setting sun and the calmness of the water. Why were they doing it?'[7]

Dolphins are social and intelligent creatures, and besides the normal, smooth, slow roll in which they arch above the surface to empty and refill their lungs, they like to play. The young ones, in particular, practise aerial leaps and spins which may have a function in communication, food-herding and defence. In *Moby Dick*, Herman Melville wrote of dolphins 'in hilarious shoals which upon the broad sea keep tossing themselves to heaven'.

Bottle-nosed are not the only dolphins that visit the inshore waters. 'On Whit weekend a school of four dolphins or whales, up to four metres long, arrived in an isolated, rocky bay on the Beara Peninsula. Photograph enclosed of grey-backed dolphins, with tall, dark-coloured dorsal fin and a squarish forehead. They remained there for more than an hour, often less than one hundred metres offshore, and always in close formation. They surfaced frequently until in the far distance a boat engine started and they dived out to sea. What were they and what were they doing in such shallow water?'[8]

These were Risso's dolphins and they range from the west coast of Africa, along the west coast of Europe as far north as the Hebrides and the Shetland Islands. They are not common inshore, but we have seen them cruising northwards among the small, rocky islands off the coast of Mayo. They live generally off squid and octopus, but also eat fish. They were probably feeding in the bay where they were seen.

Whales belong to the same cetacean family as porpoises and dolphins, but they are more often observed dead on the beach than live in the water.

However, a Galway reader caught sight of some nosing around in the bay: 'They were much bigger and heavier-looking than dolphins, and were black with big dorsal fins. They were hugging the coast of Galway Bay between Barna and Spiddal, within two hundred to four hundred yards of the shore. One group of five was followed by another of four. I noticed snub noses on one or two, but they weren't jumping like dolphins so I didn't manage to see much more.'[9] They could have been killer whales which have a very tall, triangular fin, but much more detail would be needed to make a positive identification. The school could have followed a shoal of fish into Galway Bay.

Whales do not normally swim so close to shore, but another whale, probably also fishing, was seen by a boatman in Clew Bay. 'While boating along the south shore of Clew Bay in August, I spotted a large animal which I took to be a whale. It was thirty to forty tonnes and fifty to sixty feet long. The tail was at least six feet wide and white underneath, as were the flippers. But it was behaving peculiarly. It seemed to be using its flippers as if swimming with an over-arm crawl, first showing one flipper, then the other. It was in very shallow water for a whale.'[10]

The most likely whale of that size and at that time of year in these waters is the fin whale (also called finback, finner, or common rorqual). A fin whale was washed up a year previously not far from this sighting. This one could have followed a shoal of fish into the bay; although a baleen whale which strains plankton from the sea, the fin also feeds on fish. When a fin whale is hunting a shoal of mackerel or herring it ascends gradually and, just breaking the surface, it rolls with its mouth open to drive the fish across its path. On these rolls, it would show its flippers alternately. Schools of fins move north along the Irish coast in spring and south again in autumn in annual migration.

The north-east Atlantic population of humpback whales also migrates in spring from winter breeding grounds off west Africa to summer feeding grounds near the north of Norway. In autumn they make the return journey. 'On April 25th with four acquaintances, I saw one of the great whales surface in the shipping channel about two hundred yards inside the mouth of Dun Laoghaire harbour. It exhaled with a loud noise, like steam being released from a pressure valve, and then submerged. A knowledgeable boatman, who got a better view when it surfaced at the bight on the east pier, identified it as a humpback. It was so big I think it must have been a fully-grown adult.'[11] Humpback whales are up to fifty feet in length and ungainly in shape. There skin is rugged and bumpy, and they have long and narrow flippers, with irregular knobs, which are almost one-third the length of their bodies. Their usual migration route is inshore, sometimes hugging the coast along the west of Ireland and Scotland. If one appeared in the Irish Sea, it was some way off course. There are minke whales in the Irish Sea, but they are about half the size of the humpbacks.

Another humpback visited Glandore harbour in west Cork on the return migration. 'Towards the end of June, while I was hauling lobster pots off Adam Island, outside Glandore, a very young humpback whale surfaced beside my fifteen foot boat and stayed right beside me for the next four-and-a-half hours. It followed me between offshore rocks that are quite close together, and into coves only fifteen feet deep, and when I stopped it arched its spine, put its tail down vertically and stayed under the boat.

'I was able to rub its head beside the blow hole, and once I managed to put my hand down alongside its mouth. I got a good few blasts in my face from the blow hole; they had a faint fishy smell. It was almost twenty-five feet long; the side flippers were about eight feet, white on top and bottom, and reached back level with the dorsal fin. The rest of the body was grey or black with some barnacles, the most noteworthy were a group of eight on the tail. It followed me ashore (but not into the dead-end coves even though it could not see the end), then turned very fast and gracefully. It was a most intense and moving experience.'[12]

The young humpback probably thought the boat was part of its pod, and adopted the position of a calf to its mother which is alongside her flank. At 25 feet the juvenile humpback was little more than a year old, and while it was able to forage for itself, it was still breast-feeding. It may have thought that it could suckle the boat when it performed its tail-down flip under the boat.

It is always a sad sight to see whales dead, deprived of their dignity and decomposing on the shore. We had our first encounter with a dead whale here on the shore in 1983, and it turned out to be a rarity: a True's beaked whale, five metres long. Previously there had been only three authenticated strandings in Britain and three or four in Ireland. Then, in a peculiar turn of fate, another turned up on a local beach in 1987 making the Viney score two and the Irish total six. There have been other local strandings of dead whales: the sperm whale washed up on the beach in the 1940s, from which we salvaged a vertebra out of the sand some years ago; and another decomposing whale on the rocks in 1995. Here is Michael's description of it at the time: 'The forty feet of sperm whale, flukes ten feet across, all lying limp as a lost evening glove, were not the easiest object to measure without the risk of slipping into the corpse's clammy embrace. Somewhere under the great mass of the head, with its lopsided blow hole, were jaws lined with teeth like goose eggs. I have always wanted a row of those for my window-sill, but this was not the occasion.'

Another fairly rare whale was reported by a Co Clare reader, who sent a photograph. 'This mammal was thrown up on the western strand at Seafield, Co Clare. I have borrowed three books from the local library and cannot identify what species it is. Also, local fishermen, old and young, have seen nothing like it before. It is twenty-five feet long, twelve feet in circumference and toothless.'[13]

The mystery mammal, beaked like a dolphin, was a female Cuvier's whale. Despite the fact that it appeared to be toothless, it was, like the True's beaked whale, one of the toothed whales of the Ziphiidae family, which catch squid as their main food. The teeth are confined to one or two pairs in the lower jaw of the male, and in the female are embedded in the jaw and invisible. This Cuvier's whale washed up in Clare was the second that spring, another was beached in Co Sligo.

The principal features which the observer should look for when trying to identify whales and dolphins are: the estimated size; the size, shape and position of the dorsal fin; the shape of the head, flipper and tail; the colour and markings; behaviour - whether they jump clear of the water; and in whales, the position of the blow hole, the height and direction of the blow and whether it is single or double. In beached cetaceans all the measurements should be taken, and it should be noted whether whalebone, or alternatively teeth, are present in the mouth.

Eye on Nature had a request for the identification of one very unusual beached sea mammal. 'My nieces and I discovered this creature at the mouth of a small stream near Sybil Head in west Kerry in January 1995. It had obviously been washed ashore by the heavy swell. We notice that the tusks were not pointed, had they been cut off?'[14] The accompanying photograph showed a large seal-like animal, with two tusks, lying upside down and semi-submerged in shallow water. The tusks positively identify it as a walrus, and as these are used mainly for raking clams from the sea bed, they get worn and broken in a long life. Walruses are not seals but form a family of their own. They live near the Arctic Circle in the North Atlantic, but in winter they move southwards and two were sighted off Donegal in the previous year.

Varieties of an amphibian reptile regularly visit Irish waters, and have sometimes been washed ashore dead. We have found the bodies of loggerhead and Kemp's ridley turtles on the tideline, and at small fishing harbours at Achill and Old Head have twice taken a measuring-tape to a great leatherback, fatally entangled in fishing gear and brought ashore. *Dermochelys coriacea*, largest of the sea turtles, does not have the tough, horny carapace of other species, but a smooth black skin raised in seven parallel ridges the length of its body, like the stretched, tarred canvas of a currach. A reader sent a photograph of one she and her family came across on Ballytrent beach near Rosslare in 1991.[15] But a Dublin reader met a leatherback at sea. 'I was sailing in a race in the Glandore regatta, West Cork, in mid-August, when we heard a splashing off the stern. To my amazement I saw a huge turtle surfacing for air. My skipper, an experienced ocean sailor, informed me that it was a leatherback, and the biggest he'd ever seen. It was about six feet long and three or four feet wide. I didn't know that these mysterious creatures came so far north.'[16]

Nine feet is the usual length of an adult leatherback this would have been a juvenile. The turtle regularly migrates to our shores from the Caribbean, following the drifting shoals of jellyfish on which it feeds. It is a protected species, and if found alive entangled in nets or ropes, should be considerately released to complete its round trip back to warmer waters. One expert correspondent, Gabriel King, who studies turtles in Irish waters, suggests that it may not just be an occasional migrant:

'The thermo-regulatory adaptations of this unique animal enable it to survive in the north-east Atlantic even as far north as the Faroes and possibly beyond. My own work shows an increase of leatherback turtles in recent years. What is also emerging, contrary to general belief, is that the occurrence of apparently healthy adult/sub-adult chelonids, sea turtles with a horny carapace, suggests positive presence rather than accidental meandering.

'For several days in 1989, on the south-east coast, a leatherback turtle was seen making repeated attempts to come ashore, returning to the sea at the approach of people. Stirrings, perhaps, of a dormant, primeval instinct, finely tuned to climate change, in a creature that has outlived the dinosaurs by sixty-five million years.'[17]

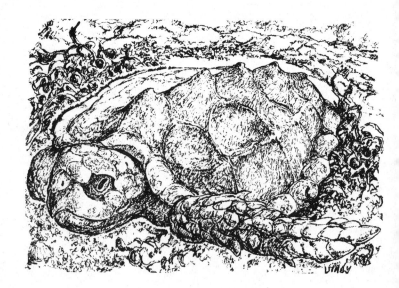

ELEVEN

SO BRIGHT THEY WOULD CUT YOUR EYES...

 When a small, unsolicited box arrives in our post these days, it is treated with caution more appropriate to a letter bomb. We have had a wide variety of insects and their larvae delivered like jewels in well-wrapped matchboxes, jiffy bags, polystyrene packaging and, kindest to us, transparent pill boxes. But when it comes to insect reports and sightings, the living butterfly is always left to flutter on. The brilliant and easily-recognised red admiral gets more column inches than any other.

The red admiral is not, of course, strictly an Irish butterfly: it is a resident of Europe, particularly around the Mediterranean region and as far north as 48 degrees latitude, which crosses France at Orleans. Large numbers move northwards in spring and arrive in these islands in late May and June - only as immigrants, or so it was thought until recently. Much of the correspondence to *Eye on Nature* has been taken up with attempting to disprove this conventional wisdom, with some very interesting observations. Over ten years it has become very obvious that some red admirals hibernate in Ireland, perhaps even as pupae.

In 1988 a Clonsilla observer saw a red admiral butterfly on the Royal Canal at Ashtown on April 24th.[1] On February 10th, 1989, one was seen at Dalkey.[2] 'On March 28th, 1989, a sunny day, but with a cold north-west wind, we were delighted with a visit from a red admiral butterfly, which alighted on the terrace and remained with wings outstretched to the sun for about five minutes. It stayed around the garden for some time, flitting from wallflower to wallflower. It appeared in perfect condition. The red markings were a deep orange in colour.'[3]

One was seen at Rostrevor in Co Down on January 8th 1990, undoubtedly a hibernating butterfly lured out by a warm sunny day.[4] In

1994 a red admiral 'in good condition and flying strongly' was seen near Castletown in Wexford on April 4th by the earlier Clonsilla observer.[5] And on April 14th, 1995, a Mayo observer saw one 'in pristine condition as if it had just emerged from a chrysalis. It could not have been an early immigrant as the wind had been from the north.' In 1996 the same observer saw, on June 17th, 'the first red admirals, brand new and so bright they could cut your eyes'.[6] Then: 'On March 26th 1997, I saw a red admiral butterfly which lacked lustre. Could it have over wintered or was it an early migrant? We had southerly winds then for over a week.'[7] As a worn specimen it was more likely to have hibernated as an adult.

Those in 'pristine' condition could conceivably have over-wintered as pupae and gone on to hatch as adults early in the year, but there is no scientific proof of this happening, and in their European habitats the butterflies hibernate as adults.

Certainly, all but a very few of the red admirals seen in Ireland migrate here in summer, lay their eggs on nettles, hatch into caterpillars, pupate and emerge as butterflies in roughly two months. It is this new generation which flies back to southern Europe in the autumn. Weather conditions affect their numbers, and in the late 1980s many local populations crashed. However, while observers were writing to *Eye on Nature* reporting their scarcity in 1989, a remarkable episode in Irish butterfly migration, and a valuable record of red admiral migration south in autumn, arrived by way of the British Butterfly Conservation Society.

On September 29th an English naturalist, Cliff Christie, and his wife Joyce, both wardens of a nature reserve in Oxfordshire, were visiting Ireland and went to Galley Head, near Clonakilty, Co Cork. It was a beautiful, very warm day. They were invited to visit the lighthouse, and as they drove the last hundred metres, between high walls, they found red admiral butterflies basking on the stones, 'at first ones and twos, then tens, and before long they were rising off the walls like swarming gnats'. They stopped the car and walked back to find the butterflies now restless, many still on the walls, many more on plants on the cliff-top and others heading out to sea. Mr Christie was convinced that there were at least five butterflies per metre on each wall, giving a total of about a thousand. By noon the next day they had all gone.[8]

To complete the red admiral cycle of migration, a Limerick reader witnessed their inward movement from the continent in 1995: 'In late

June, during the first spell of really warm weather, we were on Banna Strand in Co Kerry. There were quite a few of largish, dark butterflies which were coming in from the sea and travelling inland so fast that no markings could be seen.'[9]

Another summer visitor is the painted lady butterfly. As plane loads of holidaymakers head south from Ireland to tropical resorts in spring and early summer, flights of painted ladies wing through Europe from north Africa to feast on our flowers and rear a new generation. Though not as plentiful as the red admiral, the painted lady sets out earlier on the northward migration and reaches Ireland in May or June.

In 1988 they arrived early to Waterville, Co Kerry. 'On April 26th, I saw my first painted lady butterflies. There were lots of them flying about the roads.'[10] One was seen in Co Wicklow on May 24th in 1992[11] and even earlier in 1994. 'On April 30th, near Kilmichael Point, on the borders of Wicklow and Wexford, I saw two painted lady butterflies sunning and flying together. On May 2nd, near Kilmore Quay, I saw one painted lady. Their appearance coincided with my car being covered with Saharan sand.'[12] These records are important in the study of painted lady migrations.

In 1995 we had a convention of painted lady butterflies. They appeared again on June 17th 1996. Of the two I inspected closely, one was quite faded and the other in full perfection. Thus, in prevailing north and easterly winds, it made me think that they must be breeders. Is this recorded?'[13] In their tropical habitats painted lady butterflies do not hibernate: they breed continuously and, as far as is known, do not survive the winter here in either egg, larval, or pupal stage. The breeding cycle is approximately forty-six days, so it is possible that a very early arrival, say around the first of May, could have produced a new generation.

1996 seemed to be a good year for the ladies, there were several reports of sightings from all around the country. 'For the first time in nearly fifty years we have painted lady butterflies. There seem to be more butterflies than usual this year. Our orange buddleia has been covered with peacocks, red admirals, small tortoiseshells, one small, brown butterfly, possibly a dingy skipper, and one painted lady. A neighbour who has white and purple buddleia had at least three painted ladies.'[14]

Whether a year is good or bad depends not just on conditions here, but also on the size of the first brood of the butterfly in North Africa. If there is a big hatch of spring caterpillars there, and they eat almost all the sparse vegetation, then the butterflies that emerge move northwards, and these are the painted ladies that find their way to Ireland in early summer. They breed here and their progeny return south in autumn. They do not survive the winter here because, according to one theory, they don't have enough sorbitol in their blood at any stage in their life cycle. Sorbitol is the insects' anti-freeze agent, present in the butterflies which do survive our winters.

The earliest sighting reported to *Eye on Nature* was on March 28th 1996, near Lismore, where the observer had seen lots of painted ladies in the previous August.[15] There have also been March arrivals at Killarney National Park. In many years, indeed, the butterflies only manage to reach the south of the country, and they are too few, or the food is so plentiful that they do not need to travel further afield.

Clouded yellow butterflies are fairly regular summer visitors to Ireland, but like the painted lady, they often only reach the south and south-east coast; only in exceptional years, when great numbers arrive at these shores, do the venture further north, so few people have seen them. For those who haven't, the male is a deep yellow colour with dark marginal bands on the upper side of the wings and black spots on the underside. The female is a lighter yellow and both have an orange spot in the centre of the hind wing. They belong to the same family of butterflies as the small and large white, the cabbage butterflies, the orange tip and the brimstone. The caterpillars, which emerge in August, are emerald green and are found on clover, vetches and other legumes; and the chrysalises are yellowish-green.

'On May 24th 1992 I saw twelve clouded yellow butterflies near Kilcoole, Co Wicklow. I caught five of them, three females and two males, and I hope to get eggs. I understand that there have been reports of clouded yellow butterflies in the north of Ireland.'[16] Obviously a good year for them. Another report noted 'clouded yellows in abundance spotted at Dublin Airport' on May 13th 1997.[17]

Eye on Nature had regular reports on our three common immigrant butterflies, red admirals, painted ladies and clouded yellows, and 1992 saw all of them here in plenty: 'The exceptional invasion of migrant butterflies in the Dublin-Wicklow area deserves to be put on record. Between May 20th and 26th I saw twenty-two clouded yellow butterflies.

They were laying their eggs, for preference, on birdsfoot trefoil, in fact, to my amazement, one laid on a few poor plants of it near my back door here in Blackrock. I also saw more than twenty painted ladies and seven red admirals.'[18]

The peacock butterfly is the most flamboyant of our native species. Its pairs of 'eyes' look fierce and frightening to any bird contemplating it as a snack, but add particular beauty set in the rich, warm red of the wings.

It is widespread throughout the country, yet there have been years when it crashed, due to wet, cold seasons. A wet summer can limit the new generation and a harsh or stormy winter can kill hibernating adults. The end of the 1980s saw the peacock butterfly greatly reduced in many areas, but there was a slow recovery in the early 'nineties. One correspondent had not seen a single peacock butterfly in his Co Wicklow garden[19] and another wrote that it had almost vanished from the Glencree valley,[20] but in August of that same year two biologists from Dublin Corporation saw six of them 'busily feeding on two lone stands of hemp agrimony' beside the River Tolka near Finglas.[21] Later reports showed that local pockets had survived in Co Clare,[22] at Straffan, Co Kildare,[23] at Clonmel, Co Tipperary[24] and that they were so abundant on the islands in Lough Mask 'that the number could hardly be counted'.[25] By 1991 a general recovery had taken place and reports came from far and wide that the peacock were on the wing again.

When they emerge from hibernation, peacocks mate and the female lays her eggs on nettles in April and May. The velvety black caterpillars are slow growers, so there is only one generation each year. The butterflies emerge in late July or August, and these hibernate to produce a new generation in the following year.

Like the peacock, the small tortoiseshell butterfly hibernates as an adult, mainly in buildings. In houses it often hides itself in the folds of curtains, and where there is central heating the butterflies sometimes emerge in winter, thinking that spring has come. 'Around Christmas I had a butterfly fluttering on the French windows. I put him on my hand and opened the door but he did not fly off. He remained inside, fluttering about light fittings. I did not think they survived through the winter.'[26] These hibernating tortoiseshells are the second generation, hatched in August and September from the butterflies born in spring. As noted earlier, wrens sometimes invade their winter quarters and eat them, and bats and spiders prey on them too.

One Dublin correspondent had a remarkable encounter with tortoiseshells when hill-walking. 'On August 20th, walking in the west Wicklow hills, we witnessed an apparent hatch of tortoiseshell butterflies in numbers unprecedented. Some four miles of our route lay through flowering purple heather, and this was exclusively populated by resting, pollinating or sky-spiralling tortoiseshells. By late afternoon their density must have been many hundreds per acre. The sight will remain my most vivid memory of an exceptional summer.'[27] It was not a hatch, as tortoiseshells lay their eggs on nettles, the food plant of their caterpillars. The butterflies were drinking nectar from the flowering heather, and 1995 must have been an especially good year for them.

There was a similar report from Co Down in 1991: 'On September 22nd, the amazing number of one hundred and fifty plus small tortoiseshell butterflies was recorded at Newcastle. The largest number of tortoiseshells reported in a single garden this year was ninty-four at Omagh.'[28]

The prevalence of the caterpillars' food plant determines the presence of any butterfly species and the size of its population. The red admiral, peacock and small tortoiseshell all lay on nettles, and most butterflies have evolved in close association with particular native plants or plant groups. The lovely marsh fritillary, for example, depends on devil's bit scabious, and the brimstone butterfly on buckthorn. One reader helped to make the point after a visit to the Midlands: 'On one of those delightful summer days in June, I visited Mongan Bog near Clonmacnoise, where I saw possibly thirty butterflies and a few moths fluttering about the heather. An hour or so later I visited Birr Castle Gardens, with its magnificent display of exotic flowers, but didn't see as much as a single butterfly.'[29] The peat lands have one special butterfly, the large heath, whose food plants are sedges, cotton grass and other grasses. Generally speaking, butterflies and moths occur where their native food plants grow best, and gardens such as those at Birr have usually been planted with flowering trees and shrubs from distant ecosystems. This is not to say that butterflies necessarily disdain the nectar of exotic blossoms: buddleia, after all, comes from China!

Some fast-flying butterflies can be difficult to identify on the wing and those that fold their wings when they settle can compound the problem. 'At the end of July, while walking along the bank of a stream, I saw a collection of about five or six beautiful green butterflies. They flew from trees to plants on the side of the stream, and their camouflage was incredible on the different plants. Were they green hairstreaks?'[30]

The letter did not give the size of the butterfly, or say whether the green was light or vivid in colour, or whether it referred to the upper or lower side of the wings, or both. It is also important to know whether the butterfly rests with its wings open or shut. The green hairstreak is brownish-green on top and vivid green underneath; the female brimstone is a pale, lemony, green and both of these rest with their wings closed and blend in with the leaves of plants. The dark-green fritillary rests with its wings open but the upper wings are speckled brown, while the underwings have dabs of green and white; and the silver-washed fritillary is similarly speckled brown on top, with a light green and silver wash underneath. On balance, the butterfly which the reader saw could have been a green hairstreak.

'On August Monday I saw two pairs of the lovely fritillary butterfly feeding on the blossom of blackberry briar. From my book it would seem to have been the dark green fritillary, although the only green it had was a tint on the top of its head tapering towards its back. Its wing expanse was two to two-and-a-half inches. The colour of the wing was a dazzling orange-brown with a mass of dark spots. The lighter male or female was distinctly bigger and its underparts were of a pale colour.'[31] The wingspan is right and the female dark fritillary is larger and paler than the male; both have pale underwings dabbed with green and white.

'Recently I saw butterfly which I have never seen before. The wings were two-thirds to three-quarters white with one bright orange portion.'[32] This one was a male orange-tip, the female does not have the orange spot. It belongs to the same family as the cabbage whites, the nemesis of all vegetable gardeners. But, while the caterpillar of the orange-tip also feeds on plants of the Cruciferae family, generally mustards, cuckoo flower and charlock, it does little damage because the eggs are laid on or below the flower on the chosen plant, and the caterpillars feed on on the seed pods.

The 'cabbage' butterflies are more properly called large and small white; the other whites do not trouble the vegetables. Whatever gardeners feel about the cabbage whites, schoolboys may be curious. 'Evan Power and Conor Breen brought in a caterpillar. Soon it spun a cocoon. It looked dead. Evan brought it home for the holidays as we thought it would be too cold in the classroom. After the holidays he brought it back. Then one day a cabbage white emerged. Its wings were wet and crumpled, but soon they dried out. We released it on our Kanzan cherry and there's one thing for sure, it's a well-educated butterfly.'[33]

There are only three blue butterflies in Ireland, the common blue, the small blue and the holly blue. But the common blue looks uncommonly like the adonis blue which is a European butterfly and not found in Ireland. 'In August we came upon some delicate blue butterflies, with a paisley pattern on the underwing. They were fluttering around flowers on the dry banks of the Dodder. We looked them up and thought they were adonis blue, but the book says that they are absent from Ireland.'[34] And another correspondent also mistook the common blue for the adonis when she saw them on Inis Meáin in the Aran Islands.[35] The dark edges of the wings are more pronounced in the adonis blue, but the definitive difference lies in a small cell-spot on the under forewing of the common blue.

Finally, one pair of enthusiasts caught the final stages of metamorphosis when a butterfly emerges from the cocoon. 'My son and I are watching caterpillars with the usual excitement. This year we managed to catch the elusive moment when the caterpillar pupates and sheds its skin. It hangs from the leaf for about twelve hours, getting thinner at the top, there's some great change going on. The skin then splits at the head and the pupa wriggles out of it. When the last segments are reached, there's great twirling and tremendous effort until the empty skin falls to the ground. Then it hangs for the next ten or twelve days when we watch with further wonder at the emergence of the butterfly.'[36]

Of the twenty-eight species of native butterfly, three common migrants, and six rare migrants and vagrants in Ireland, not more than half-a-dozen are recognised by the general public. However, *Eye on Nature* has a few butterfly enthusiasts who send regular reports of a wider range of species. Apart from those given above, there were reports which came in of green-veined white (actually the most common butterfly in Ireland but lumped together with the large and small white as just 'white' butterflies), speckled wood, meadow brown, small copper, wall, grayling, holly blue and ringlet.[37] This left unreported: the dingy skipper, wood white, brimstone, brown hairstreak, purple hairstreak, small blue, pearl-bordered fritillary, marsh fritillary, gatekeeper, and small heath.

A *'Millennium Butterfly Atlas'* is being produced by two UK voluntary groups, Butterfly Conservation, and the Biological Records Centre.[38]

NOTES

TWELVE

ELEPHANTS AND HUMMINGBIRDS

Moths join the butterflies in the Lepidoptera, the order of insects characterised by wings with overlapping scales. Hawkmoths, sometimes as large as butterflies, attract a lot of attention as adults and as caterpillars during the summer months. Like the butterflies, some of them are migrants.

They are large, generally fast-flying, often colourful, elegantly marked insects, with long, pointed, hawklike wings; and the caterpillars are equally large and just as striking. Hawkmoth caterpillars, with a few exceptions, can be recognised by the 'horn' on the end of their abdomen.

The elephant hawkmoth, a large pink and gold moth with pointed, back-swept wings, is a resident distributed all over the country, and observers are often surprised at the size of its caterpillar. 'In mid-September, near the Maharees in Kerry, I saw a creature vaguely like a hairy Molly crawling over the sand hills. It was about four inches long and one-and-a-half inches in circumference, divided into ten segments with two suckers instead of legs, and two circles, like eyes, per segment. It was smooth, not hairy, and had a semi-pointed head. It was greyish-black in colour with a greenish-yellow tinge. When I touched it, it drew in its head so that the front was now formed by the first segment with the circles looking just like eyes.'[1]

This hawkmoth gets its name from the trunk-like snout of the caterpillar, one observer described it as 'a snout like Fungie'[2] which it retracts in a defence posture as described above, thus expanding the size of its body and and enlarging the eye-spots. The caterpillar generally feeds at night on willowherb, bedstraw and bogbean, and in gardens on fuchsia. The moth is on the wing at the end of May and can be seen at dusk flying around these plants.

A smaller version, the small elephant hawkmoth, is also a native although perhaps not as plentiful as its larger relative. It has more gold than pink on its wings and body, and its caterpillar lacks the abdominal horn. 'On June 15th I was surprised to find a small elephant hawkmoth feeding on some sweet rocket in my garden. I've never seen one before and wondered was it a migrant.'[3] The adult moth feeds on nectar-producing plants like honeysuckle and rhododendron and, as noted above, sweet rocket.

The poplar hawkmoth is another resident that is on the wing in May. It is a large, slow-flying moth, with broad, scalloped wings, that sometimes comes in open windows at night and flies around disconcertingly, bumping into things and people. 'At the end of May I saw a large moth about one-and-a-half inches long from the tip of its horns to the end of its tail. The horns were about five-eighth of an inch long. At rest it was two-and-a-quarter inches from wing-tip to wing-tip. The front wings were less than half the size of the hind wings, all brown-grey in colour and ribbed. The front wings were partly under the hind wings. The head was grey brown, the body brown, tapering to the tail which had an upward turn at the end.'[4]

The hind wings of the poplar moth project in front of the forewings at rest and are often mistaken for the larger forewings; the 'horns' were, of course, its antennae. Its colour can range from ash-grey to pinkish-brown, but the projecting hind wings and the upturning tail are the clinchers for identification.

'In July I came across this large insect on clothes hanging on the line: a moth with black and white and pinky-orange striped body, grey thorax with two black spots at its base, wings patterned grey and brown. It was a very warm, sunny afternoon and the insect was very lethargic and would not move off the clothes. I put it in a covered bowl for a few hours and then when I gave it a nudge it flew away. It was about three inches long, and when in full flight its wing span was about five inches.'[5]

It was a convolvulus hawkmoth, a summer visitor from Africa that arrives in June, a night flier, not often seen, which in this case was lying up during the day. This moth has a very long proboscis, actually longer than its body, which it uses to drink nectar from sweet flowers such as honeysuckle, tobacco plants and petunias. When not in use, this proboscis is coiled under the head. The caterpillars of the convolvulus hawkmoth are very large, up to 11 cms or four-and-a half inches long, with oblique stripes; they feed on convolvulus leaves, hence the name, but almost never reach maturity in this country as they rarely survive the winter. In some years these moths reach only the south of the country but they have been recorded from every county.

Even on a first encounter, one species of small hawkmoth simply insists on its identity. 'Early in June on a warm sunny evening we noticed a large insect hovering over a clump of catmint which was in full bloom. Its wings were beating so quickly that they were visible only as a blur. It was about three centimetres long and light brown in colour with black and white tail feathers. The head seemed tapered ending in a long proboscis. Could it have been a hummingbird hawkmoth?'[6]

If its wings were visible the forewings would be seen as dark brown with black markings, and covering the golden brown hind-wings. The hummingbird has been the most reported of all the hawkmoths, not least because it flies during the day as well as at night. It is another visitor, this time from southern Europe, and hovers with quivering wings as it probes for nectar in a variety of sweet flowers; petunias, sage, valerian, pansies, lady's smock, tobacco plants and catmint, among others.

'While out walking in mid-June at Hook Head in Co Wexford, I came across dozens of hummingbird hawkmoths on the sea thrift and cow parsley. The weather was warm and sunny, and the following evening there were only a few around. Is it unusual to see them in great numbers, as I have only seen a single one before?'[7] It's rare to come across such an arrival of hummingbird hawkmoths from the continent; they were probably resting after their flight.

They usually have two broods here if they arrive early, one in June and a late one in September or October. In its more southerly territory this hawkmoth hibernates as an adult, but only very exceptionally do any of the late-hatched moths survive the Irish winter. They can arrive quite early in spring. 'On April 19th I noticed a hummingbird hawkmoth moving in and out of the primroses and aubretia. Is this exceptionally early for such a moth to arrive? I would like to attract more of these very attractive insects to my garden. What plants provide a nursery for the larvae?'[8] The caterpillars feed on bedstraws and wild madder, but the nectar-producing plants listed above will attract the convolvulus hawkmoth and the hummingbird as well.

There have been no reports to *Eye on Nature* of the death's head hawkmoth, also a regular migrant from Africa to Europe. Named for the skull-like marking on its purple thorax, it comes here in most years and has been recorded in all parts of the country. The body is striped black and yellow with a blue line running down its length; the forewings are frilly patterns of various browns, while the hind wings are striped like the body. In resting position the wings are held over the body like a roof.

The caterpillar is also a handsome beast. 'In early September we found an unusual and beautiful caterpillar in one of our pighouses. It was three-and-a-half inches long, apple-green underneath shading to a yellow upper, with seven purplish, oblique stripes down each side with some spots on top. It had a rough, yellow horn, and there were black spots on the face. We think it was a privet hawkmoth and when we gave it privet leaves to eat there seemed no doubt.'[9]   A photograph was enclosed, and was certainly that of a young caterpillar of the death's head hawkmoth: an important observation, because only a few are recorded each year.   In captivity, as it happens, the caterpillar is often fed privet leaves.

More than five hundred of Ireland's largest moths are listed in the standard handbook *A Revised Catalogue of Irish Macrolepidoptera* but only a handful have been recorded in *Eye on Nature*. The subtle beauty of these insects is suggested by some of their names: burnished brass, royal mantle, small argent-and-sable.

A particularly fine photograph of a moth was sent by a Co Waterford reader who thought it might be a 'giant emperor moth'.[10] It was actually the larger female of the emperor moth, a most striking insect of our heathery moorland. The giant peacock moth which is sometimes called the giant emperor, and which strongly resembles the emperor moth, is a southern European species, the largest on the continent. It never reaches these islands. Another photograph of 'a black and pinkish moth which was one of hundreds that collected around the outside light'[11] proved to be that of a cinnabar moth, more closely described by another observer: 'When walking on Inishbofin, Co Galway in June I saw several insects which I never saw before. They were about half-an-inch long with furry, black bodies and long, black antennae. They had black, gauzy wings with largish, red dots, which folded back when they landed on wild flowers; when they were flying the wings looked completely red.'[12]

The cinnabar moth likes open, sandy areas along the coast and lays its eggs on ragwort, or *buachallain*, which the caterpillars devour voraciously. Its forewings are bluey-black with pinky-red dots, and at rest they fold over the hind wings which are a beautiful shade of magenta. Cinnabar moths are largely nocturnal and congregate in large numbers at lights, but they often fly by day.

The six-spotted burnet can, at a casual glance, be mistaken for the cinnabar moth; it flies by day, but is found in flowery meadows where knapweed and scabious abound. The larvae feeds on trefoils and other leguminous plants. 'When walking on the cliff near Coumeenole, Co Kerry, we came across a colony of six-spot burnet moths. There were many cocoons on the long grasses, and many of them had what seemed to be dead moths half-emerged from them. We wondered why they were dead. Was it the cold weather?'[13] They might not have been dead. Burnet moths have a peculiarity: the pupa partly emerges from the cocoon before the adult moth escapes.

A Donegal reader sent a photograph of insects that had 'very dark, green wings and red spots' which he saw near Rossnowlagh and again near Ardara.[14] They were also one of the many burnet moths, six-spot or five-spot or *Zygaena lavanduli* , all of which have red spots.

There are moths flying all through the year, but it can sometimes take a lepidopterist to recognise a cold-weather moth for what it is. 'The scarce, early spring moth, the pale brindled beauty, has never been recorded in Kerry. This year, 1988, for the first time since I came to live in Killarney elevin years ago, I saw a female of the species on my windowsill. Females are rarely seen as they are wingless.'[15] Pale brindled beauties belong to the large family of geometers, so-called because their larvae are 'earth-measurers', called inch-worms in America and loopers or stick caterpillars here. As they travel, they arch their bodies into a loop between one movement and the next, as if measuring out the distance. Motionless, they can be quite invisible, being camouflaged as twigs.

The winter moth, another geometer, flies from October to February and the female is also virtually wingless. A Dublin reader rescued a male of the species from a puddle in the second week in January. 'On close inspection', he wrote, 'it is quite attractive although appearing drab at a distance'.[16] This is the case with many of the smaller moths. 'In early September my mother saw a tiny caterpillar like a twig on the clothes line.

It was about an inch long and greyish brown.'[17] This was the caterpillar of one of the geometers, probably the garden carpet moth.

And another geometer: 'Early in summer I saw a beautiful butterfly or moth near the curtain in the living room. It was two inches by one-and-a-half inches, pale lemon yellow, had two broad wings with two vertical, brown, shadow lines on each wing. The wings ended in two pointed spurs with red-brown spots. The head was yellow, furry and extended in a V down the body.'[18]

It was a swallow-tailed moth which is attracted to light and regularly comes into houses. It flies in July to August, and lays its eggs on the leaves of hawthorn, elder, ivy and privet. The stick-like caterpillar feeds on the leaves of the host plant and hibernates through the winter, feeds again in spring, pupates in June and the moths emerge again in July.

The bordered white moth is a looper that can be a serious pest in conifer forests. 'On a visit to Co Clare I noticed a green caterpillar about three centimetres long feeding on a pine tree. It was a type of conifer well adapted to the seaside location, and a plague of caterpillars had eaten quite a lot of the needles. Because the needles smelled so much of turpentine I could not imagine that this tree could be the preferred host of any caterpillar.'[19]

After the looper, the sprawler. 'A moth called the sprawler, from the characteristic pose of its caterpillar, is common in the south of England but quite local in Ireland and not often seen. Much to our delight we saw our first specimen just before midnight on November 5th at an outside farm light. The sprawler is on the wing in November and early December. and often does not appear until after midnight. The moth was recorded at Athy, the writer's home, by the Rev Keith M Dunlop, Rector of Athy in the 'twenties and 'thirties. My son and I are particularly pleased to find this species surviving in spite of the "high tech", insecticide sprayed, cereal and sugar beet cropping which completely encircles our farmyard.'[20]

It takes a sharp eye to spot a sprawler, since it's a dull, speckled moth that disappears altogether when settled on the bark of a tree. It belongs to the noctuid family of moths, so-called because they are all night-fliers. The bright green caterpillar, in its defensive posture, is stretched out with its head and thorax thrown back, hence its common name. The same observer also caught a common wainscot moth in his mercury vapour light trap.[21] It is another noctuid moth whose caterpillars feed on grasses.

The figure-of-eight belongs to a group of moths called prominents, because of the tuft of hair on the hind edge of the forewing which sticks up on its back when the insect is at rest. It is found mainly in the northern half of this country, but our Athy lepidopterist found one in his hawthorn and blackthorn hedge in late October when it lays its eggs. The caterpillars feed on these two bushes.[22] Although otherwise of sombre, but subtle, colour, the moth has an unmistakable figure of eight on its forewings.

'When I was cutting some overgrown grass in June a pure white, winged creature flew out. It was about the size of a very small moth but the shape of a dragonfly, with long, narrow, very slim, with two slim wings on either side. It looked as if it had been dipped in whitewash.'[23] The winged creature was the white-plumed moth, a dramatic-looking insect even though it is numbered with the group called micro moths. It flies in June and is found where there is bindweed to feed its yellow and green caterpillars. Instead of two wings on each side, it has five feathery plumes, hence the name. The wings are generally rolled around each other at rest and held at right angles to the body like a slender T.

Another observer found a related one at rest: 'A strange moth appeared on our landing. It completely folded its wings into cylinders of the same size and thickness as its body at rest, with the wings standing up at an angle to its body. It was beige in colour, 1.5cm in length, and had a slender, uniform body like a stick insect.'[24] This was *Agdistis benetii*, which has no common name, another plumed moth but, incongruously, its wings are not divided. It is found in coastal areas particularly on salt marshes.

A micro moth which is an acute household pest made a guest appearance in *Eye on Nature*. 'I have recently suffered a plague of moths. They seemed to like a particular woollen blanket, and showed uncanny skill at inserting themselves into the spaces between books. With wings folded the moth was thin, with a cinnamon/silver sheen and a trace of pinkish spots, and the head had two white patches, one on each side. Could this be the mother of all the bookworms?'[25] This was one of the clothes moths, probably the tapestry moth, which has a white head. The case-bearing clothes moth is also cinnamon-coloured. The caterpillars of clothes moths and the brown house moth cause a lot of damage to household fabrics, clothes, feathers and hair, because they are able to digest the keratin found in animal fibres; they will also consume cotton fabric and cereals.

The caterpillars of moths are often much more striking than the adult insects themselves. Each one is distinctive, although one might think that all hairy mollies look alike. 'I saw a bronze, furry caterpillar in August, with about five or seven yellow and black, upright tufts all along its spine. It had a black head with feelers and a black tail.'[26] This one sounds like the caterpillar of the dark tussock moth which is about in August and feeds on a wide variety of shrubs and bushes. It is not widely seen in Ireland.

'I found a caterpillar, green in colour, with deep velvety-black in the divisions of its segmented body. It had three white tufts on its back like a military helmet, and an orange-red tail tuft at an angle. Placed in a cigarette box for observation it promptly spun a fine, silken cocoon and vanished from sight.'[27] We hope the correspondent kept it safely and put the cocoon in a glass jar in spring, when he would see a pale tussock moth emerge, very hairy, with feathery antennae. It lives in woodland and the caterpillar feeds on birch, oak, elm and other deciduous trees.

'I saw this exotic caterpillar on the outside of the house. It was about three inches long, a little thicker than a pencil and had pincers on its tail like an earwig. Its belly was green shading in parts to dark brown on its sides. A narrow white band ran along its sides near the back which was light brown. The head was brown with a black band and an orange band around the neck; there was a further orange band, about one-sixth of an inch, across the upper back.'[28] This was the caterpillar of the puss moth which feeds from July until September on deciduous trees like willow and poplar, and takes on a fierce appearance when disturbed. The head rears up and puffs out, the tails wave red filaments, and an acid squirts from a gland behind the head, all this for a small moth with the soft, silvery charm of a tabby kitten.

A Co Mayo observer sent in a photograph of a twig on a tree covered over its length with a fine web like a cobweb.[29] And a Kildare reader 'came across a strange dense mass of cobweb swathing the roadside hedge for some fifteen to twenty feet.'[30] These were the silken tents of a colony of caterpillars, of either the lackey moth or the ermel moth. After hatching, the young caterpillars cover a branch of their food plant, hawthorn, sallows, apple, and others, with this web-like tent and feed underneath its protection. They extend the tent to cover more and more of the branch as they need new food supplies. Sometimes they sun themselves outside the tent. They can do a lot of damage to apple and plum trees and are found abundantly in the Burren.

The lackey moth belongs to a family called eggars which are found all over Ireland. 'I saw recently the biggest caterpillar I have ever seen. It was surely three inches long, with light-brown hairs and dark-brown body, with white flecks down both sides. It was feeding on a briar leaf. I could actually hear it munching off sections of the leaf.[31]

This was the caterpillar of the oak eggar moth which, by a biological quirk, has two sub-species with different caterpillar appetites and reproduction cycles. The southern sub-species feeds on a wide range of trees and shrubs, including the oak and also the briar, so the above report, from Dublin, seems to be of that sort. The northern sub-species, on the other hand, feeds on heather and bilberry, and its adult moth turned up in Co Kildare: 'I was surprised when my grandson produced a large, foxy-coloured moth which he found in our farmyard. It was a northern eggar and a particularly good specimen. To me this is an unusual moth for this country. The specimen found was of large wingspan, coloured bright russet brown, with a bright golden spot on the wings.'[32]

To end the moths, a shared moment of contemplation. 'In the kitchen late one night I saw what appeared to be a baby worm, suspended by a single thread of a spider's web, midway between the table and the ceiling. Fully extended it measured about one inch. While I watched, the worm gyrated while being slowly propelled upward without a spider in sight. Reaching the ceiling it slowly made its escape towards the wall.'[33] It was the caterpillar of a moth, spinning its silken cocoon.

NOTES

THIRTEEN

MYRIAD MANIFOLD AND MULTICOLOURED

 'I confess to a liking for wasps,' wrote Robert Lloyd Praeger, the great Irish naturalist, 'they are so active and daring, dainty and cleanly.' But most people still, it seems, attribute to the wasp a malevolence it certainly does not deserve.

For most of the summer, wasp workers are too busy collecting insects and caterpillars to feed to their young to bother with humans; they hover near people only in late August and September when they have finished their brood rearing. Then, relieved of their chores, they embark on a sugar-eating binge, before they die with the onset of cold weather. They are only interested in settling on a human who is in some way smeared with something sweet, and will sting only if they feel threatened. However, this reader's tale does have some moments out of Hitchcock:

'There was a time when I just disliked wasps, but that was before they invaded our home. The wasps built their nest high up in a dark corner of the coal house, and flew in and out at the top of the garage drainpipe. All summer long they worked on their home until it resembled a large Chinese lantern. My fears gradually receded; I began to admire their dedication and hard work.

'Then, one day towards the end of August, I painted the garage and coal house doors. That night, with my husband away, I woke in the small hours and got up to see the time. I went into the kitchen and switched on the light. Fiercely buzzing and whining up and down outside the window were literally thousands of wasps. Even as I watched, they began getting in through a slight opening.

'One of the girls remembered that the woman next door had a spray, and she woke her up to get it. She stuck her arm around the kitchen door and sprayed the hordes within. After repeated doses we heard the tip-tap of bodies falling all over the kitchen. Later, an expert friend was of the opinion that the strong smell of the paint prevented them from finding their way home by scent. They gathered nearby and when the kitchen light went on, the globe looked like the nest and they made for it.'[1]

Readers, if not enamoured with wasps, are always intrigued by their nest-building. 'While out walking at the end of July, my curiosity was aroused by a noise from a hedgerow: it was as if two dry sticks were being rhythmically tapped together. I was amazed to find that the maker of this sound was a wasp. It was tapping away at a dried hogweed plant. If it was gathering fibres for pulp what was it using to bore with?'[2] The answer is her strong jaws; only females are the nest-builders. July was a bit late for building, but the queen was still laying and may have needed more space.

Some nests are enormous. 'Football size is big for a wasps' nest, but one I removed this winter from between the rafters of a garage was at least two feet high and a foot wide. Every year I watch wasps taking wood scrapings from doors and windows, but this was remarkable workmanship. The outer three to four inches were beautifully laminated, and a large sack filled with the nest weighed only about a pound. The bottom tier of cells had held mainly queens, a couple of hundred of them, so this year could be busy.'[3]

The two everyday wasps of Ireland look very similar, but have slightly different markings, and while they can both build very big nests indeed, there are differences between them. The common wasp uses pulp from rather rotten wood and makes a nest with a sometimes rather brittle finished envelope in mixed shades of white and browny-yellow. The German wasp always uses sound wood, to make nests of relatively tough, grey paper. The final layer always contains the new queens as they are the last to hatch in late August; the previous layer contains the males who are hatched in late July.

The tree wasp is slightly smaller than either the common or the German wasp, and it builds a much smaller nest which it hangs usually in a tree or bush. One Dublin reader found one, 5cm in width with an entrance hole half-a-centimetre across.[4] Another reader found three in his attic, of about the same size, very fragile, with a texture resembling very thin cardboard.[5] These nests hold fewer than one hundred and fifty individuals.

On learning what the nests are, many people want to destroy them. 'In mid-July we removed from the ceiling of our garage a wasp's nest which was teeming with bright yellow wasps both inside and outside. We placed it in a plastic bag in a field close by. Several minutes later, the wasps returned to the original nest base, via an open window in the garage. Frantically they tried to rebuild the nest from its original base working very hard. Gradually their zealous movements became more sluggish and within two days, their colourless corpses dropped from the ceiling and lay strewn on the ground. Did the wasps need the nest material for their survival?'[6]

An account to touch the hardest, wasp-hating heart. The wasps needed the nest itself in order to survive. The nest was the work of hundreds, perhaps thousands of wasps, several generations of workers that had built it in layers. The workers' job at that stage was to feed the larvae with chewed up insects and caterpillars. Their cycle was broken and they put nest-building above foraging for their own survival.

But wasps do have some considerate neighbours. 'While clearing a side flower-bed recently, we just avoided disturbing an underground wasps' nest at the back, with its tiny entrance at the wall. We are fascinated and have put up protective stakes around the nest area, where the soil is slightly humped and has an aerated appearance. Our unintended invasion has in no way upset them, so we would like to know when the colony will disperse for the winter, allowing us to dig the nest up and examine it. Or should we leave alone for future inhabitants?'[7] Both of our common species of wasp nest underground, or under cover such as in an attic or shed roof. The nest, however is abandoned in autumn, October, to be safe, and not used again, but a variety of animals and birds, including badgers, pine martens, squirrels, frogs and beetles, will scavenge it for dead larvae and insects.

Because they feed their young on animal protein, wasps are an asset in the garden, helping to control the population of insect pests such as caterpillars. They don't sting, but bite their prey. 'I saw a common wasp attack and kill a hover-fly much larger than itself. It then swiftly decapitated its victim and flew off with the head.'[8] The wasps themselves, feed only on nectar or other sugary liquid, which they get from flowers, damaged fruit or a jam-pot left open; they also feed on a type of syrup that is secreted by their own larvae.

'In the early days of August I have noticed several of what appear to be queen wasps on the wall of the house, and a couple inside as well. They appear rather lifeless, are large and have the usual yellow rings on their bodies.'[9] These are the male wasps, hatched out in late July and hanging around waiting for the new queens to hatch.

When the young queens are mated in September, they disappear into their winter quarters and do not appear until spring. Then the workers go on a sugar-eating spree, which is when they become a nuisance. When the cold weather comes the males, old queens and workers all die. 'On a visit to the Blessington Lakes at the end of October, we saw that some large beech trees near the shore had been felled. We noticed a circle of wasps all around the outer part of one freshly-cut tree stump. They looked docile and did not move when we approached.'[10] They were either stoned on sweet beech sap or dying.

Some wasp behaviour in the long, hot summer of 1995, observed in two different locations, offered an arresting demonstration of the appetite for sugar, both in wasps and butterflies. A reader in Co Meath found a willow tree in her garden buzzing with wasps, and later a dark, burnt-looking patch appeared on the grass beneath the tree and attracted red admiral butterflies in great numbers. 'The butterflies packed themselves on to every available space on the blackened patch of grass with their wings outspread, tips touching, so that the whole patch was covered with shimmering colour like a tiny piece of oriental carpet. At one stage I counted twenty butterflies, with others hovering nearby.'[11]

The phenomenon, with its explanation, was confirmed by a reader in Killarney: 'The young branches of a willow were covered densely with dark-grey aphids, which were all ejecting honeydew, at quite a rate, into the air. A large number of wasps were feasting on it, catching it in mid-air or sucking it from the trunk of the tree. Beneath, on the grass, a large dark patch had formed, from the honeydew, where many red admirals were feeding, with the occasional peacock or tortoiseshell.'[12] Honeydew is the excretion of surplus sugar from the sap sucked out by aphids. In a wasps' nest, the grubs being fed on insect protein secrete a surplus of sugar in their saliva, which is licked off by the adults.

Each year, usually in August, we get letters describing a large insect that looks like a particularly heavily armed wasp, or sometimes a box in the post, enclosing one. This is the horntail, also called the wood wasp, which is a 4cm-long sawfly and not a wasp. The female has a long ovipositor in a yellow sheath which she uses like a drill to bore holes in conifer trees, in which she lays her eggs. The larvae take two or three years to mature before they emerge as winged adult. The grubs sometimes survive the chainsaw and the carpenters' tools and emerge as adults in newly built houses, to the concern of the occupants.

It is normally a harmless insect, but one correspondent had a different tale to tell. 'This bee or wasp gave me a very sore bite through the back pocket of my denim jeans double thickness. It was quite sore for several hours but left no trace of a bite. I was up a stepladder clipping a leylandii hedge.'[13] We are tempted to conjecture that, busy egg-laying among the conifers, the wood-wasp mistook the taut curve of denim (perhaps the pocket had a brown leather brand-patch?) for the trunk of a tree.

The male wood wasp is rarely noticed, as it flies around in the sunshine at the tops of the trees in conifer woods, but one observer saw one. 'In mid-August we had an insect visitor to our garden. It sounded like a loud bee but with an added sound like rustling, dry paper. It looked very fierce, about seven centimetres long with a spike at the end of its orange-rust coloured body. It had stripes on the upper half, and bright, lemon-yellow spots on the head, and the same coloured legs and antennae.'[14] The spike at the end of its body is short and not at all as fearsome-looking as the ovipositor of the female.

'Recently I noticed a sizable insect resting on a leaf. Its length from head to tip of semi-transparent wings was three centimetres, wings overlapped the abdomen tip; colour mainly black with chestnut, some yellow at top of abdomen; the antennae were five to six millimetres with pale yellow clubs; it had fairly large, muscular legs. Was it a robber fly or a type of wasp?'[15] That was a precise description of a birch sawfly, which is larger than the honey bee. Robber flies have very short antennae and they are not clubbed. It is a fast-flying insect which buzzes loudly and is found in wooded areas where its larvae feed on birch leaves.

The larvae of other sawflies are pests in the garden, like the turnip or the gooseberry sawfly. The little green and white larvae of the latter can strip all the leaves off a gooseberry bush in May in a matter of a couple of days.

There are many insects that cause problems for foresters. 'While chopping some firewood, on one piece I noticed a blister about an inch or more long. I couldn't pick it off so I sliced it with the hatchet, thinking it was part of the timber. Underneath I found a most ugly looking grub with a number of large rings or scales that were hinged. It had scooped out a little hollow in the timber, and had built the blister over itself with the pieces.'[16] It was probably the larva of a pine weevil, a beetle-like insect that causes great damage to pines and spruce. The larva burrows into unseasoned wood.

Beetles are more often encountered on the ground than flying; but most of them can fly, and often do so at night. 'In our sitting room a large beetle-type insect was flying around. I caught it in a towel to put it out. It was a biggish black beetle with clubbed antennae and a pair of orange chevrons on its body. There were a number of small brown insects crawling on it, too.'[17] Several beetles have parasitic insects. This was one of the sexton beetles which the next correspondent watched at its work. 'I saw a large, black beetle busily burying a dead bird the size of a thrush, leaving only the tops of the tail, wings and legs above ground. I presume that it was trying to save its body from other scavengers. Was this for consumption or for egg-laying?'[18] The aptly named sexton beetle buries small carcases for both purposes. A pair of beetles find the carcase, mate and then bury it by scooping out the soil from underneath it. The female lays her eggs in a small passage leading off the burial chamber, and remains there to feed the offspring with regurgitated food until they are able to feed off the carcase.

'We found huge numbers of the enclosed insect [beetle, 1.2cm long, black thorax, brown elytra] flying clumsily over beaches at Glasilaun, near Renvyle, and at Mannin Bay. Most died at the edge of the sea or on the sand. We wondered if they were attracted by water, as they were also concentrated along the little stream at the back of the beach. They were harmless, but so numerous as to be a nuisance.'[19]

The insect was a scarab or dung beetle called *Aphodius fimetarius*, which is a common species. However, the phenomenon described is unusual behaviour. The chafers, which belong to the same family as the dung beetles, sometimes swarm on foraging expeditions, and swarming could also be caused by a population explosion. Another beetle, similar to the scarab, visited a Co Wexford correspondent. 'In autumn a large beetle flew into my workshop, hit the light and landed upside down on the bench. He was brown underneath gorgeous, metallic, green wings. In the small crevices and folds of his underbody tiny mid-brown insects, almost like fleas but much smaller, moved about freely.'[20] The dor beetle is also known as the lousy watchman because it is often infested with mites.

One family of beetles are vegetarian and the bane of gardeners' lives. These different chafers feed on various trees and shrubs, and the larvae feed on the roots of a wide range of plants and crops. The cockchafer, also called the maybug, is the most notorious.

One correspondent saw a couple of swarms, 'thousands of insects' of either summer or garden chafers in Muckross demesne over beech trees.[21] A harmless member of the same family engaged the interest of a Dublin visitor to the Burren. 'A friend and I came on some insects in the Burren the like and beauty of which neither had ever seen. They were about the size of a thumb nail, with a slightly bronzed neb on the back of the head, and bright, iridescent, metallic-green wing cases. The first one was sitting on a hummock of plants, and others were flying about low near the ground. Then we saw others leaving and entering the hummock although there was no apparent hole.'[22]

They were chafer beetles called *Cetonia cuprea* which have no common name but, if they had, might be called copper chafers. The observer probably came on a hatch, because the larvae live in ants' nests. They are fairly common in suitable habitats throughout the country. Another Dublin reader wrote to say that one didn't have to go to the Burren to see them as they were plentiful on the privet hedge in her garden; she also has a number of ants' nests.[23]

'Every summer my garden is invaded by tiny bugs. They have bright scarlet bodies and reddish-brown wings. In flight they drift through the air, bodies almost perpendicular to the ground. When two of them meet up on a hazel or shasta leaf they bonk enthusiastically. Are these little creatures soldier beetles?'[24] We, too, have hordes of soldier beetles in the garden; they feed on the insects that visit flowering umbelliferae, such as meadowsweet and yarrow. They are sometimes called 'bloodsuckers' because of their colour, but are quite harmless.

The devil's coach-horse, or *deargadaol* in Irish, is a rove beetle which feeds on slugs and the larvae of insects and is the gardeners' friend. 'I found a beetle, 4cm long, under a bath mat in Co Mayo. Attempts to capture it caused it to arch its back and move its tail over its back like a scorpion.'[25] While the black *deargadaol* may look threatening it does not sting.

Much sought after to take up residence in gardens are the various ladybirds, and the summer of 1989 was a particularly good one for them. 'Is there such a thing as a plague of ladybirds? On an evening walk on a field near my house, literally every blade of grass had a ladybird. I have never seen so many.'[26]

Plague is a word better saved for the aphids on which the ladybirds had been feeding. The population explosion of aphids, which arose from the previous, very mild winter, meant a high survival rate for ladybird larvae (they each eat several hundred aphids), and a greater number of ladybird generations.

Every year since the first *Eye on Nature*, the great diving beetle has made a regular appearance in the column. 'People think I'm joking when I tell them that the great diving beetle and its larvae have been decimating the goldfish in my garden pond. I have ordered another half-dozen golden orfe, but I'm not too hopeful. I did notice that the goldfish did not suffer last year until the tadpoles had begun to leave the pond, so all might be well until August when the fish might be big enough to defend themselves.'[27]

The appetite of *Dysticus marginalis*, 35mm long, sleekly olivaceous, yellow margins to its wing cases, is certainly no joke. It is common in garden ponds and ferociously carnivorous, munching up to forty tadpoles in a day. It is often the mysterious assassin of ornamental fish. The larvae are long (up to 60mm), multi-segmented and even more aggressive than the adult. When people wonder what has happened to their tadpoles, the great diving beetle has undoubtedly taken up residence in their pond.

There is another garden insect that is sometimes mistaken for a colourful beetle. 'I found a bug between the bricks of our incinerator. To save it being fried I lifted it off but it made no effort to fly. When I looked later it had disappeared. It was about one-and-a half centimetres long, bright green with what looked like brown wings in a Y-shape on its back. It had six green legs, brown antennae, and a permanent lean forward from wide shoulders, so that its small head was difficult to see. The only thing like it in my insect book is a green shield bug which is stated not to appear until May.'[28]

The insect is a shield bug, but sounds more like the hawthorn shield bug, because of the brown Y on it back. It was hibernating in a crevice of the incinerator. The green shield bug becomes bronze before going into hibernation and only turns green again just before it emerges. Shield bugs are also called stink bugs because many of the species release a pungent odour when in danger. There are huge variety of bugs, all with mouth-parts adapted for sucking the juices of plants or animals.

The other common denizen of the garden, blamed for damaging flowers, is the earwig; but it does little harm and cleans up a lot of debris. Its main fault is its abundance and a liking to stay pressed up against a smooth surface, which is what moves it to hide among the petals of flowers like dahlias, or in among the crevices of cauliflowers. This Dublin observer saw one behaving in a peculiar manner. 'On a sunny day, a female earwig, *Forficula auricularia*, described one-inch circles, anti-clockwise on the garden path for over an hour (about 1,500 times). She looked healthy and I use no chemicals. Curious to know if she was wafting pheromones I placed a male beside her, but after two revolutions he fled! Have you any insights on this behaviour?'[29] It was not normal behaviour and may have resulted from a damaged antenna, eye or leg which disoriented it. On the other hand, it may have come from a garden where chemicals are used.

Among the brightest wings of summer are those of dragonflies and damselflies, also called demoiselles. Apart from their gorgeous iridescence, observers often note their very large eyes. 'While sitting by a river on my father's farm I saw some dragonflies which were blue-bottle in colour. They had four wings which seen in another light looked green. One landed on my hand and I saw that it had enormous black eyes and big mandibles, and that its legs were covered with tiny hairs. It danced about in the air and seemed to be playing with another insect which was the same shape but of a dull, brown colour.'[30]

This dragonfly was a male common hawker, *Aeshna juncea*, common in this country; the brown one was a female, and they were performing a mating dance. The eyes of the this family of dragonflies have up to thirty thousand facets and they can see in almost all directions. They feed on a variety of insects and also on butterflies, discarding the wings. Hunting often on the wing, dragonflies catch their prey with legs which have spines for the purpose, and then tear it apart with strong mandibles.

The difference between the various dragonflies lies to a great extent in the colour pattern on the head, thorax and abdomen. They need careful examination while alive, as the colour fades on many of them when they are dead. Dragonflies and damselflies belong to the same order of insects but to different sub-orders, and they have some physical differences. 'Along the Dawros River in Connemara lives what in flight appears to be a dragonfly, but when it rests on a leaf the folded wings seem to be leg-of-mutton shape, and the wing colour changes from navy blue to turquoise green. Quite a beautiful insect but is it a dragonfly?'[31] Only the damselfly folds its wings; the dragonfly holds its wings open and out to its sides when at rest.

The hordes of flies impinge on our lives mainly as a nuisance; we tend to forget that as scavengers they perform a service, cleaning up decaying matter. Like the sexton beetles the larvae of blow flies help to clear away carrion. 'How many bluebottles will breed out of one dead mouse? The dead mouse cannot be reached inside the wall, and bluebottles emerge at an average rate of , say, eighty a day for the past week. What is the rate of reproduction and when will it end?'[32] The eggs laid by one bluebottle vary according to the food supply, but can often weigh more in total than she does. They hatch within a day or two, the maggots grow for a few days more, and the pupa releases the adult fly a few days after that. Each female hatched will go on to produce several generations while the food supply lasts.

The bluebottle is a blow-fly and has several less attractive relatives. 'A peculiar fly visited our garden in August. The head section was very bright, almost "day-glo" pink or cerise, while the body section was a sort of pale-blue turquoise. Both sections had a shiny, metallic lustre. It was about one centimetre long. and three millimetres wide.'[33] This was probably the greenbottle, which varies from bluish-green to emerald. Its eggs are often laid in cuts on sheep and cause problems for the animal. It can be found on carrion, dung and flowers everywhere. The pink head section is a pair of very large eyes.

Hover-flies are the ones that sometimes imitate bees and wasps in their appearance or hang in the air, bright as little jewels, before darting to a new position. The larvae of many of them feed on aphids, but some are found in very strange locations. "After filling in a brick-lined hole in the ground, the bottom of which was filled with sawdust, leaves and various debris, I poured a three-inch bed of cement. The next day I found fifty or so grubs [sample enclosed of grey grub, 2.5cms long, with a vertical whip-like, tail about 3cms long]. Two or more holes seemed to show where they came up."[34]

The grubs, aptly termed rat-tailed maggots, are the larvae of a hover-fly, called the drone fly because it resembles the drone of a honey bee. These larvae feed on decaying matter in stagnant ponds. The long tail is, in fact, a telescopic breathing tube like a snorkel.

The real honey bees, originally natives of southern Asia, live in colonies and their social life revolves around the colony's single queen. As she is unable to forage for herself, the queen is always surrounded by her faithful attendants, except when she leaves the hive for her nuptial flight with the drones. A colony may number from ten thousand to fifty thousand worker bees, which build a wax comb of six-sided cells, some of which are nursery cells and others used to store honey. The queen lays thousands of eggs which are sealed in individual wax cells; when the larvae hatch they are fed by nurse workers. Other workers feed the queen and yet more store honey to feed the colony during the winter.

The life of the hard-working, worker bee is short, and many die during the working season. Even so, towards mid-summer, the hive becomes too crowded with new young bees, so new queen cells are developed and from these one new queen is allowed to mature. If the existing queen is still strong the new queen departs the hive with a swarm of attendant workers to set up a new colony. When a swarm from a bee-keeper's hive flies off to start a fresh colony in the wild, it may select the corner of an old building, a hole in an old tree, a chimney or an attic.

'A swarm set up a colony a few years ago in the roof space of a flat-roofed extension to my holiday cottage in Connemara. As the house was only occupied for short periods during the year, the bees were no trouble, until the ceiling began to sag. A local bee expert was commissioned to get them out, and this meant cutting a hole in the ceiling. To everyone's dismay the colony was much larger than anticipated, and the amount of honeycomb so colossal that a successful removal was impossible and the bees had to be destroyed.'[35]

Some swarms that set up independent colonies in the wild have been unlucky in other ways. In another holiday house, a reader found a densely packed pile of dead bees in a disused chimney, killed by cold, hunger or disease.[36] At Cranagh Castle in Co Tipperary, bees returned twice over a period of years to a wall cavity where they had lived. A bad summer wiped them out in the mid-Eighties and a couple of years later a swarm arrived and took up residence again. In 1995, the castle, and the colony, were destroyed by fire, but 'two years after our house was burned, in a fire hot enough to melt lead, bees have returned to the same place on the same wall where they had nested for years. Perhaps some melted honeycomb remained in the mortar of the wall, or a race memory brought bees back to the same location.'[37]

Honey bees are social insects, but there are many different solitary bees whose queens make nests in the ground or in walls or cavities, provision them with honey, lay eggs in them and fly off. Although solitary, they often build their individual nests close to each other. 'Some months ago I placed a heap of grass cuttings at the base of one of my rose bushes. Lately I have noticed wild bees to-ing and fro-ing to three little holes at the bottom of the mound. May I expect to be rewarded with a honeycomb in due course?'[38] Our correspondent would have been disappointed; there would be no honey, the larvae would have eaten it all.

'Sitting out in my back yard, I saw a bee fly by carrying a portion of leaf. I followed its flight and it disappeared into the keyhole of a lock on a shed door. I watched for some time as it flew back and forth, each time bringing a portion of leaf. On examination, I found that the bee had manoeuvred a portion of leaf into the position of a chute at the bottom of the keyhole and was carrying each portion up this avenue. What was it doing?'[39] This was a solitary, leaf-cutting bee which uses portions of leaf to construct sausage-shaped nest cells, often in a hole in old wood. The keyhole was just the right size for her purpose.

Bumble bees are also social insects and build nests where more than a hundred will live and work together. They have much the same social structure as honey bees, but the activity of their queen is different. 'On March 12th I came across a bumble bee on the road outside my house. At first I thought it was dead but it was still moving sluggishly. I brought it in and fed it a mixture of honey, sugar and water which it took eagerly. It was the first time I had seen a bee's very long tongue. I put it outside and it disappeared but returned later for more food.'[40] This queen bumble bee had just emerged in a weakened condition from hibernation. The young, mated queens are the only members of the bumble bee family that survive the winter. They emerge in spring to feed on pollen and nectar, select a nest site and then lay eggs. The queen then feeds the first hatch of larvae which become workers, who then feed all subsequent hatches. Males and new queens are produced in late summer.

'In mid-October I was fishing in a small boat about a mile out from Greystones when about noon I was buzzed by a huge bumble bee for about five minutes. Then it gave up and took off, aiming straight out to sea for Wales!'[41] Bumble bee queens are much larger than their workers, and the queen of *Bombus terrestris*, which is the largest of the species, certainly has a huge presence. The ocean-going bumble bee was a looking for a place to hibernate, and may have been attracted to the fisherman by a bright colour; they are very fond of blue.

Industrious ants are not a householder's favourite tenants. 'Noticing a small swarm of ants uncomfortably close to the house, I sprayed them from a can of Cooper's Fly and Wasp Killer. To my amazement they immediately sprouted huge wings. But their activity was not immediately affected, and I was reduced to stamping them out.'[42] These were ants assembling for their mating flight. Another observer did not interfere. 'A nuptial flight of ants erupted from my garden and spiralled up into the sky. Looking up I was surprised to see black-headed gulls behaving like flycatchers, hovering and darting after the winged ants. Above them the Dublin swifts were also swooping on the feast.'[43]

In summer the worker ants rear males and queens, all with wings, but keep them underground until the time of the nuptial flight. One of the wonders of this phenomenon is that all the nests of a particular species release their sexual ants into the sky at the same time. This may be done to prevent cross-breeding and to swamp the appetites of predators. The triggers for the nuptial flights are climatic, including high humidity. The males die soon afterwards, but the mated queens return to earth, rub off their wings and go back underground, there to lay eggs for the next ten or twenty years.

The formic acid sting of an ant is mild compared to the bite of a mosquito of which there are eighteen species in Ireland. 'There is a biting insect at large in this area which is causing large, hard, intensely itchy swellings with a small blister at the centre. The bites remain swollen and irritating for a week or more and seem immune to all the usual remedies. It is very small, about 3.5mm long, has a long, very thin extension from the nose or mouth, and dark-brown spots on the abdomen and wings.'[44]

The description fits *Culliseta annulata*, one of the native mosquitoes, which is 7-8mm long, double the length of the one mentioned above. It is known to cause blisters and severe inflammation, but does not seem to carry disease. There are other mosquitoes in the same family which may be the culprit. Four species of anophelines, some of which have brown spots, are also found here; these are the mosquitoes which are capable of transmitting malaria. Although they bite humans regularly, malaria rarely results; perhaps they are not carrying the malaria parasite or it has not developed sufficiently.

Midge is a name applied to small flies and gnats belonging to several families. Not all of them are biting insects. 'Sycamore trees near my house have large, plate-like, fungal growths on them which I occasionally knock off. Recently I noticed little white grubs, about half-an-inch long, emerge from them, make their way to the edge and jump into space.'[45] Bracket fungus plays host to many insects and their larvae, particularly springtails, fungus gnats and some beetles. These grubs sound like the larvae of springtails. There is a symbiotic relationship between the larvae and the fungus: they increase its temperature, causing convection and movement of air around it, which helps disperse its spores.

'Could you identify a tiny black insect, one millimetre long, which I find regularly on books. Is it a book louse? If they are harmful and damage books what can be done to prevent them? They also seem to thrive on wicker work. They seem to move very fast, and I sometimes see their young.'[46] The tiny insects are, indeed, book lice, parent of the little worms that burrow in books printed on certain types of paper. They live on the minute moulds and fungi that form on books or woodwork in even slightly damp conditions. They do not usually cause much damage, and the most efficient way to get rid of them is to eliminate the damp by dry heat, or fires, or the use of a dehumidifier. They are very common indoors in Ireland because of the high humidity.

Another unwelcome guest in Irish houses in the past was the house cricket. With tongue firmly in cheek, one reader regretted their passing. 'Where have all the fire crickets gone? Years ago around the countryside one could hear the constant chirping of the crickets, nowadays not a chirp. Does anyone know where one could get a few to introduce them to a house?'[47] And if you killed one, the others would come out and eat holes in your socks! Of course, that was in the days of open-hearth fires, and socks drying on the crane. The house cricket, *Acheta domesticus*, has not disappeared; in old houses it has merely retreated to other crevices created by central heating and stoves. We are quite sure that we hear cricket song in the chimney enclosing the outlet of our wood-burning stove; but the cricket is unlikely to have colonised new building estates or new houses.

An exotic immigrant which has become a resident is the smooth stick insect found in south-west Kerry. 'While visiting neighbours in Derryquin, near Parknasilla, on June 18th, they drew my attention to an insect on the wall of the house. I immediately recognised it as a stick insect, mainly from watching wildlife and tropical programmes.' A few weeks later the same observer reported that the original stick insect had vanished but a smaller one had appeared on the same wall. It had a very faint greenish tint like a twig that had not quite died. Was it a baby?[48] It could have been a young one, but it could also have been the male of this particular species, always smaller than the female. Smooth stick insects have been living in several of the more sheltered, humid corners of the south-west for a century or more, introduced, possibly as eggs, with the planting of trees and shrubs from New Zealand and other southern Edens.

Although often grouped with them, spiders are not insects; they are arachnids, one class among the arthropods which also include centipedes and woodlice. There were no arachnophobes among the correspondents to *Eye on Nature*. All their letters were curious about the different species of spider and their cobwebs. 'A small spider jumped on to the newspaper I was reading, and then jumped again and was gone. It was about 12mm overall, black with white body markings, and with three white bars on its head which made it look like a skull. The jump or hop was about six inches each time.'[49]

It was the zebra spider, *Salticus scenicus*, the only jumping spider likely to be seen in this country. They hunt like cats and pounce on their prey. They have phenomenally good eyesight, having four large eyes like headlamps in front, and four smaller ones further back on their carapace. They are found in houses and gardens, and often catch the eye on sunny walls.

'I found a strange, large, very white spider on some white daffodils, and later on white wallflowers. He refused to be moved to the yellow daffodils.'[50] This was a female *Misumena vatica*, no common name but fairly common in these islands. Her colour can also be yellow or pale green depending on what flower she adopts. She is one of the crab spiders which lie in wait on flowers for their prey.

The house and shed spiders are the ones that frighten people because of their size. 'I have a huge, black spider in my garden shed. The spread of its legs would cover a £1 coin. Would its bite and that of other Irish spiders be dangerous, and how big is the largest Irish spider?'[51] The black spider is probably one of the *Amaurobius* family which live in garden sheds; they have no common names. *Amaurobius similis* is brown with black mottling and is about 12mm when fully grown. *Amaurobius ferox* is very dark, almost black, and grows to 16mm. A large spider could pierce the skin but the bite would be no more irritating than a nettle sting. The largest Irish spider, brown with a strong pattern on its back, is *Tegenaria gigantea*. The female lives for some years and reaches 18mm in body-length.

Cobwebs are fascinating constructions, and even the most common ones are considerable works of architecture. But it was the webs that covered large areas of grassland that engaged readers of *Eye on Nature*. 'In the Phoenix Park, what I took to be the low winter sun reflecting off waterlogged ground turned out to be an infinity of strands of silk stretched across the grass as far as the eye could see. Close by, they shimmered in the sunlight like a moonlit sea, and as I watched I saw additional strands drift along over the ground until snagged on a blade of grass. What creature in such abundance created this phenomenon?'[52]

Each strand has been extruded by a tiny gossamer or money spider, members of the Linyphiid family, which used the lifting power of an updraught from sun-warmed ground to take an aerial excursion. Millions of these minuscule aeronauts go 'ballooning' in the autumn and early winter. Their individual threads are woven together by the breeze and they ultimately drift down to cover the ground with a silken canopy. Usually this is invisible, but dew or mist can make it gleam and shimmer.

Blanket webs are also made by another member of the Linyphiid family, *Linyphia triangularis*. 'While driving in the Gortahork area of Donegal in November I came upon a field largely covered with quite thick cobwebs. What is the explanation for this phenomenon and is there a common name for this occurrence?'[53] These webs are domed and densely woven, and are supported by a complex scaffolding both above and below the sheet. When dew settles on them they become convex. The spider is twice the size of the tiny money spider, about 5-6mm, and hangs upside down from the lower surface of the sheet. When insects fall on it the spider bites the prey through the web.

'A nest of tiny spiders, about two hundred, have hatched out on an external glass pane of a porch. They are a species I cannot identify. The abdomen is bright yellow with a large, black, centre marking.'[54] After hatching out in early summer these creatures are only spiderlings and may take until spring to reach full size. Spiderlings are miniatures of the adult and this description fits exactly the unique colours of *Synaema globosum* , a small spider (female 8mm; male 4mm) which is not on any Irish record, but is common in north-west France. All kinds of unrecorded spiders arrive in this country as stowaways with various imports and modes of transport.

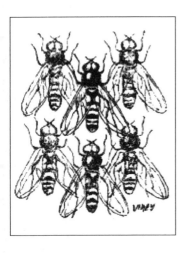
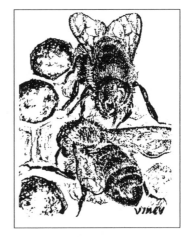

NOTES

FOURTEEN

ORGIES IN THE POND

The spring mating orgies of frogs can bring a note of real excitement to the letters that reach us in spring. 'It's happening again, the most incredible sight I have ever seen. I mean the converging of hundreds of frogs for the annual spawning. We have come to live at the foot of the Knockmealdown Mountains near a small lake, and everywhere you look you can see frogs, singly and in pairs, urgently making their way to the lake. The streams boil with their efforts to meet a partner and fight their passage to the main spawning spot among the reeds. The driveway is a sea of jumping bodies, some nimble and light, some mated couples lumbering along as the female manoeuvres not only her own weight but that of her partner.

'At the lake, already an area the size of our kitchen is a mass of speckled jelly, writhing with couples adding more. I have seen a mink crouched on the bank with the entrails of the many frogs he has already consumed. Nearly the whole lake is alive with croaking frogs, their heads just above water, the white throats pulsating. Last year, when spawning was three weeks later, we even had frogs in the house. But what compels these congregations? Are they attracted by the sound of croaking or is there a scent undetectable by me?'[1]

This is obviously a most desirable lake from the frogs' point of view, probably because of its growth of algae as food for the tadpoles. Frogs time their arrival to match the growth of algae, and its scent is almost like a pheromone in its attraction, together with the croaking of the male frogs. It is not known what triggers the actual spawning of the large and gravid females once they reach the water; but those that arrive early are grasped by a male in the tight *amplexus* embrace, and often have to carry him around for weeks before releasing the eggs, females have literally been hugged to death.

Those that arrive later may also risk the same fate. 'I visited a local pond on February 23rd where the frogs were in great voice and there was a lot of spawn. In the midst of it I noticed five or six male frogs clinging to a larger, presumably, female one, but she was obviously dead. I fished out the orgiastic bundle and noted that each had a very tight hold on the neck, legs and middle of the female.'[2]

As the spawn is laid, the male sheds his sperm on it and the drama is over for the female; she is released, but the male will seek out another female and try to dislodge the male in possession. Unfortunate females who have not yet spawned are therefore in mortal danger. Another observer saw a *goldfish* locked in the tight embrace of an ardent male frog. She got a spoon and prised him off and saved the goldfish's life.[3]

'Do copulating frogs in a pond sit in/on the surface, on surface vegetation or are they resting on the bottom?' asks one correspondent.[4] In shallow water they may be sitting on the bottom or on pond vegetation. In deeper water they can be swimming, treading water or just floating. The breathing apparatus of frogs is such that, when out of the water, they suck air into their lungs through their nostrils, by lowering the floor of the mouth. The air is trapped by a valve in the nostril, circulated by a pump in the throat and then exhaled. This trapped air gives them buoyancy. Under water, male frogs, who hibernate at the bottom of ponds, breathe through their skin.

'The most extraordinary thing happened in my pond. I found one of my frogs outstretched on his back, white tummy up, looking rather like a little person. I asked a friend to bury him and while he had him on a shovel, lo and behold, the frog came to life, somersaulted into the pond and wasn't seen again.'[5] A rude awakening! We always thought that they hibernated on all fours.

Everyone with a 'wild' pond becomes fascinated with tadpoles and full of questions about them. 'Why does development through the tadpole stage take so long in a small number of cases? Although spawning takes place within a very short time in spring, there are still some tadpoles there in September. I have also noticed that when the tadpole develops its legs it is relatively large when compared with the young frogs. Does this mean the the tadpoles lose weight in their final development into frogs?'[6]

It can take anything from three months to a year for tadpoles to develop into frogs, depending on the weather, cold inhibits the development and the food supply. The forelegs appear in tadpoles only a few days before they leave the water, but they are fully developed under the skin and that gives them a certain rotundity. At the same time the gills atrophy and the tadpoles start to use their lungs by rising to the surface of the water to breathe.

There is also a condition known as neoteny in tadpoles, reported by several correspondents. 'On February 16th, while removing leaves from the pond, I noticed a tadpole about an inch long swimming about. Isn't this unusual for this time of year?'[7] Sometimes, in particular circumstances, a tadpole grows larger but does not develop into a frog, and can live for a year or more. It is thought this condition is caused by cold.

Many correspondents were concerned at dramatic reduction of the tadpole population in their ponds as the season progresses. 'This year there was plenty of frog spawn in the garden pond and a good development of tadpoles. In mid-summer, however, as they began to lose their tails, their numbers reduced and there are now very few to be seen. This pattern has occurred over the past two to three years. Prior to that they could be seen at this time of year as tiny frogs congregating around the edge of the pond in large numbers.'[8] It is likely that a great diving beetle or two entered the pond and they and their larvae feasted on them. Tadpoles are a handy take-away for many predators: newts, dragonfly nymphs, water boatmen and birds. They also cannibalise each other. If there were not such great numbers at the start they might not survive in any location.

Irish frogs vary in colour from a basic brown or grey to reddish or greenish yellow, all with darker blobs, but sometimes one comes across a deep purple one. 'We were excavating some Bronze Age walls near St Brendan's Well on Valentia Island when we saw two black frogs nearby on the cutaway bog. They were the colour of blue-black ink with the faintest tinges of green and blue. They seemed leaner and longer than other frogs, and one was about three-quarters the size of the other.'[9] Another correspondent mentioned an 'almost black frog',[10] but they are certainly not plentiful.

'While on holiday in the Maharees, on the north of the Dingle Peninsula, my son Peter and his friend John found a toad which ran along. It was about two inches long, with an olive-green tinge, darker warts and a stripe along its mid-back ridge of a slightly more yellow-gold tinge. It ran quite fast and never once hopped, and when released went back into an indentation at the top of a sandbank. Have we found a natterjack toad which has managed to travel over the Conor Pass from its usual home?'[11]

It was, indeed, a natterjack toad, best known from sandy banks in the Glenbeigh area, but now common on the north shore of the Dingle Peninsula, especially around Castlegregory. It is the only toad found in Ireland, and lives in the sandy coastal areas of that part of west Kerry. The natterjack's main base is northern Spain, and just how it arrived in Ireland has been a matter of debate since it was discovered in 1805. The local belief that 'a ship brought them' is a plausible answer; they could have come in sand used as ballast. Some current research into their DNA could, however, suggest a different post-glacial history altogether.

Since small boys stopped messing about near streams, newts are seldom noticed. In the past a considerable mythology and folklore grew up around them in country areas,[12] but now they have vanished into the undergrowth. 'We have had occasional glimpses of a newt in our pond. Since, so far as I know, there is no natural water pool nearer than half-a-mile away, it seems extraordinary that this little creature should have found our pond. It is already used by breeding frogs and there are lots of tadpoles. Is there any way of feeding the newts to encourage them to breed?'[13]

Because the only place most of us see a newt is in a pond, we tend to assume this is where they live. But the smooth newt (the only one we have in Ireland) spends the late summer, autumn and winter on land, hibernating in cold weather under stones or in thick grass. It seeks out a pond about the end of March, rather later than the frog, and breeds in the water, which it leaves in July when the adults and young move back on to the land. The pond provides all the food newts need; they gorge on tadpoles.

Lizards are often confused with newts, and people are sometimes surprised that they exist in Ireland. 'While walking along the the cliff route at Howth in August, I saw what I thought was a lizard sunning itself on the path. It moved in a blur of speed, but before it vanished into the undergrowth I thought it was about eight inches long and dark-greenish in colour. Could it have been a lizard?'[14] The viviparous or common lizard, Ireland's only reptile, is known to inhabit the Hill of Howth, and lives in many kinds of habitat, with sand dunes and bogland the most favoured. A current survey has gathered records from twenty-one counties, but Co Wexford has accounted for more than a quarter of them.

The lizards are occasionally seen on sunny days, basking on rocks or walls or on the drier hummocks in bogs, and they feed on spiders, centipedes, insects and their larvae. 'Eight inches' is too long: 15-18cm is closer to it. The female holds the fertilised eggs in her oviducts for about three months (hence the name viviparous) and the young hatch out at, or soon after, laying.

Nobody feels nervous of the humble, slow-moving snail, but they lead adventurous lives of their own. 'I posted a letter at our local box which is set into the pillar of an ancient gate. I found that the opening was partially blocked by what turned out to be large, black snails. Later an official from the GPO rang me to say that the letter, partly eaten, was on his desk.'[15] Snails are fond of some of the gum used to seal envelopes.

'One morning a neighbour of mine saw up to twenty snails, travelling from east to west, crossing a little used road. She had never seen such a sight before and wondered what it meant.'[16] It is known that snails have electromagnetic senses, and that they demonstrate magnetically-oriented behaviour, but its purpose is not established. Many species of snail mate in May when the weather is moist, and that may have been the purpose of their westward migration.

A photograph from an observer in Co Wicklow[17] showed nineteen small, pearl-like objects nestling in a circular cluster in a shallow depression in the soil. Perfect spheres, they formed a ring of twelve in the outer circle, six in the inside and one in the middle. It was a nest of snail's eggs. The eggs are laid soon after mating and are usually buried in the soil, or in the dark under a protecting object where the environment is moist. The eggs of most snails hatch after six weeks.

'This summer there seems to be a large number of the ordinary, big, brown snails, particularly on the walls of the house. Recently I noticed small, paler brown ones and wondered were these the offspring of the bigger ones?'[18] Young snails are like miniature adults. As they grow they add to their shells, and when they reach maturity they put a lip at the mouth of the shell. If the smaller, paler ones had this lip then they were adults, and not the young of some variety of snail. A long spell of dry, hot weather can put snails into a state of suspended animation, called aestivation. They may also find it cooler to clamp themselves high on a shady house wall.

Snail shells, particularly the small ones, can be as interesting as those of their mollusc relatives which are found on the seashore. A Monaghan reader sent in some tiny, greyish-white spiral shells, 1cm long and 2.5cms wide. 'They would appear to be parasites whose host is possibly the hazel tree,'[19] he wrote. They were the shells of a tiny land snail of the *Clausilia* family, probably *Clausilia bidentata*. The shells are usually dark in colour when fresh, but become bleached in time. These snails live in moderately moist places among rocks or in woods or hedge banks, and are widespread in these islands. They feed on algae and lichens, and hazel trees are often generous hosts to both.

Slugs, of course, are snails without shells. They do have some anatomical differences, as much of the snail's body remains permanently inside the shell, but there are similarities in their mating rituals. 'I came across two tiny, white slugs in the middle of the lawn, and was amazed to find them moving about in a ritual, up-and-down and swaying fashion. When I looked more closely they seemed to be firing darts at one another from what looked like tiny, male reproductive organs, which were situated near the two antennae. They were positioned head to tail, and they seemed to be aiming the little darts at holes in the middle of their partner's body. How could they have both male and female sexual functions and still need to mate? Is it possible that they could have feelings, as they seemed to be enjoying themselves?'[20]

This was, indeed, passion among the gastropods. Slugs and snails are hermaphrodite, possessing both male and female organs, but, apart from a few snails, they still exchange sperm with partners for reproduction. Snails, but only some slugs, also exchange 'love darts' as a stimulant to sexual arousal before intercourse. This observation was an uncommon sighting of these slugs in action.

Kerry has its natterjack toads, its stick insects and 'Lusitanian' flora, and also the Kerry slug. The correspondent who watched the pygmy shrews on the floor of a disused farmhouse (see Chapter 9) also encountered *Geomalacus maculosus*. 'Before we left for Kerry there was an article in *The Irish Times* about the Kerry slug. I thought I might look out for one if it rained. At 11.05 one evening, one came in under the door and on to the concrete floor. It was quite slim and four-and-a-half inches long before it was disturbed. The head end was spotted for about an inch, then a blur of smudged spots followed by stripes with spots in between them. We decided that it was kinder to move it out into the field, rather than post it in a box, as the article suggested.'[21]

'A tree which I pass daily often shows silver trails in the morning sunlight. Curiosity eventually took me out at night with a torch, to discover 40 slugs, up to four inches long, but mostly about two-and-a-half inches, moving eerily and steadily upwards. The slugs were perfectly mottled to the colour of the bark. But this is in the dark, so why? In the presence of what predator might this have evolved?'[22] The cryptic pattern would camouflage the slug against such night predators as foxes, hedgehogs and badgers which could capture them on the lower reaches of the bole.

Slugs in the garden are another matter, and most people have declared unremitting war on them. But one nature-lover suggested a solution to slug predation on vegetables. 'In the past our family fed turnip to slugs and snails, and consequently they left the tender young cabbages alone. Since then they have met their maker, not through pesticides, I hasten to add, but on account of one resident hedgehog family which has come on board. I urge all other suburban dwellers not to kill those little slugs and snails, nature will find its balance. Then the children of the 1990's will know what the hedgehog (*gráinneóg*) looks like.'[23]

The lowly earthworm became the subject of concerned letters to *Eye on Nature* after the dreaded New Zealand flatworm, an exotic predator, invaded Ireland with imported plants. When a North of Ireland reader declared that it had arrived on his farm[24] letters came from several counties describing flatworms that they found in their soil. Almost all of them were native flatworms which pose no threat to earthworms. The New Zealand flatworm, *Artioposthia triangulata*, which arrived on this island through Belfast about thirty years ago is, however, a serious predator, enveloping and digesting them, and has been spreading slowly but steadily through the island, often through the unwitting agency of garden centres. This flatworm is about 10mm wide and up to 60mm when inactive, and can be as long as 300mm when moving. When resting under a stone slab or flower-pot it is usually coiled like a sticky ribbon and covered with mucus which can irritate the human skin. On the upper side, it is dark purple-brown, edged with stripes of dirty-yellow flecked with brown, which is also the colour of the underside.

There are 26 species of earthworm in these islands; and about a dozen common species of roundworm or nematodes, some of which are tiny. A Sligo correspondent found an interesting specimen of the latter. 'I discovered a worm-like creature on and among the plants in my garden.

It was three to four inches long, slightly smaller than the circumference of a pin, cream-beige on one side and dark-brown on the other. It moved about by probing with one end to find a perch and then dragging its body onwards. There were two or three to each square metre, but only eight or nine in total. The weather had been wet and warm all day.'[25] These were nematodes called thunderworms. They live in the soil and may be found around the roots of weeds, where they live on beetles and other insects. Summer showers can bring them out, to snake around plants wet with rain. When the plants become dry the thunderworms return to the soil.

Another worm-like creature was better known in former times because of the use of one species in medicine. The leech might have caused apprehension in earlier generations but it is an object of interest now. 'I was surprised to see a large flatworm, which I'd never seen before, in a stream nearby. It has a sucker on the tail end and uses its mouth in a similar manner, climbing about inside a glass jar. The jar contains bits of muck, weed and water which I hope has some food in it. Fully extended it is about four inches long and about the width of a pencil. Frequently it is not fully extended and resembles a slug with the head end long and thin and actively probing.'[26]

This was not a flatworm but the horse or other aquatic leech. It was not likely to find much to eat in the jar, because it feeds on all kinds of invertebrates (insects, worms, crustaceans, etc), swallowing the smaller ones whole and sucking the blood of the larger ones. The leech's diet was confirmed by another correspondent. 'During a nocturnal examination of my garden, I found a large earthworm with a small caterpillar-like creature clinging to its tail. The creature was slender, grey and about one-and-a-half inches long, Its head was reddish-brown.'[27]

The leech having a meal off the earthworm would stay attached until it had its fill. Leeches live in water and damp areas.

FIFTEEN

STRANGERS ON THE SHORE

 As ardent beachcombers, we know that the abiding lure of the strands is the chance of being astonished now and then. A good many readers, obviously, have not been disappointed.

'On a stormy February 4th I was walking along the beach at Ballytrent, Co Wexford, when a particularly large wave brought ashore a small, pink octopus. The body was round and the size of a grapefruit; the tentacles were about four to six inches and of equal length, The receding wave swept it out before I could examine it more closely. Was this a native species or a wind-blown visitor?'[1] Another reader had a similar experience on a Dublin shore. 'While walking in a gale at Sandycove at the end of September I found what appeared to be an octopus stranded on rocks about six feet above the level of the sea. It was pink and white and had what appeared to be a pair of eyes on the top of a dome-shaped head, at least eight arms and at least twice as many vacuum-pads, the latter dotted all over its belly. Fully extended it measured six to nine inches, and two inches in circumference at its widest point. I thought they inhabited warmer waters, but it looked well able for our east coast temperatures when I put it back.'[2]

The octopus is classified as a mollusc, along with the sea-snails and sea slugs: body construction, not brain-power, is what counts in this classification. Ireland has two kinds of octopus, which occur off our rockier shores and can be found in the lowest pools in summer. Along the south coast, the more frequent species is the common octopus, *Octopus vulgaris*, found as far north as the English Channel, and usually no more than 60cm across. Those our readers met, however, were more likely to have been the lesser octopus, *Eledone cirrhosa*, up to 40cm, which is found further north than the range of the common octopus. The distinctive difference between them is that the common octopus has a double row of suckers on its tentacles, and the lesser has only a single row. The lesser is more apt to be a reddish colour, but octopuses rapidly change colour under nervous control, paling at one moment and flooding with colour the next. These pink octopuses were probably the *Eledone*, alarmed or indignant at their predicament.

A Killiney correspondent found another mollusc on the strand: 'a beautifully coloured squid, orange-pink with brown tips, in great condition, eyes intact.'[3] The head of the torpedo-shaped squid has ten tentacles, each with suckers. Its skeleton is a pen-like bone inside the back, and the scrivening metaphor is continued in the 'ink' which it squirts to confuse predators.

The closely-related cuttlefish, which lives and hunts in shallower water, exceeds even the octopus in its gift for changing colour, but uses this for very effective camouflage. All that people see of this mollusc, as a rule, is the broad 'cuttlebone', washed up at the highest reach of the tide. In 1997 cuttlebones arrived in great numbers on many of our beaches. In former years they appeared occasionally on beaches in the southern part of the country. 'On a visit to the beach at Brittas Bay, I found the enclosed shell, white, oval, brittle, porous and convex. I have been wondering what it is."[4] The bone is the skeleton that supports the cuttlefish's body; the gas contained in its pores helps to keep the animal balanced and buoyant.

The mollusc family contains, more familiarly, shellfish with external skeletons or shells, but only the more uncommon reached *Eye on Nature*. "In October, walking along the beach at Waterville, Co Kerry, I came across a rotting log of driftwood. It was covered by what appeared to be black and white mussels; these were about an inch long and the shell was white, divided into three parts which were joined by a black hinge. Some had opened and a number of feathery antennae protruded from them. They were attached to the log by long, worm-like, segmented tentacles, three to five inches long, pale yellow in colour, becoming darker brown near the shell."[5]

Stalked or 'goose' barnacles are crustaceans described by one expert as 'basically little shrimps living inside limestone houses'.[6] They have actually five chalky plates for protection and attach themselves by a gristly stalk to floating debris and to whales and ships in the open seas. The feathery appendages, used to sweep in plankton for food, encouraged a medieval fiction that the barnacles contained the young of geese, and some resemblance between the animals and the black-and-white barnacle geese of Atlantic shores has given the myth a special Irish resonance. The juicy stalk, sucked raw, is considered a seafood delicacy in some Mediterranean countries. A Co Clare correspondent, who found goose barnacles on a beached wooden pole at Seafield, pulled them off and saw that 'the thing that attached them stretched like elastic and seemed alive'.[7]

These were all *Lepas anatifera*, but another correspondent found a different species of goose barnacle. 'I found a marine organism on a Mayo beach which was not like any of the common shellfish. It was 3.5cm long, diamond-shaped and 1.5cm at the widest point. It was slate-blue and encased in a whitish shell. On the top was a knob of white sponge topped by something crumbly and black.'[8] This was another stalked barnacle, *Lepas fascicularia*, which differs from the earlier one because it makes its own float by secreting a spongy, white substance; it sometimes joins with others of the species to make a communal float. Individuals may also fasten their float to some small, floating particles in the water, in this case a blob of oil.

In late summer, the pleasure of swimmers in the sea is often dimmed by an influx of jellyfish. These are usually *Aurelia aurita*, the common jellyfish, sometimes called the moon jelly, but sometimes less common species find their way on to the sands. Jellyfish breed in July and August, and by September the young are being shed by the females, who die shortly afterwards; as they offer no resistance to tidal currents, they are washed ashore. In the early 'Nineties, with a lot of mild autumn weather, these beachings did not happen until much later, and there were many letters remarking on jellyfish strandings throughout the winter.

In 1993 and 1995 an unusual jellyfish was washed in on both the east and the west coast. 'While swimming at Mannin beach, near Ballyconneely, Co Galway, in mid-August, we saw a very large, brown jellyfish on the edge of the tide. It was at least twenty-four inches wide and had hanging tentacles of the same length. The centre of it had thick, muscled tendons. As it was washed in by the waves some of the tentacles were broken off and caused a stinging pain as they brushed my ankle. Our labrador dog got stung on her paws when she trod on it.'[9] One was also seen on the steps of Dun Laoghaire Pier,[10] another in Clew Bay,[11] and we found ourselves on Thallabawn Strand.

This was the largest known jellyfish, the lion's mane, *Cyanea capillata*. It can commonly measure up to 50cm in diameter, and occasionally a lot more. The tentacles contain powerful stinging cells, and their length is actually four to five times the diameter of the bell. They fall in a curtain and are used to trap and immobilise food.

'While I was walking on Bettystown strand on October 18th, a very large jellyfish was being washed in by the rising tide. It was probably two feet across, clear in colour and had a purple ring around the edge of the crown. Underneath it was pinkish, but instead of long filaments it had short tentacles at the end of which there was what looked like a webbed foot or paddle.'[12] The *Rhizostoma pulmo*, is also called *Rhizostoma octopus* because it has eight fused mouth arms through which it filters seawater for the plankton on which it lives. It does not have filament-like tentacles around the edge of the bell, and what looked like tentacles under the bell, were these mouth arms. In the adult jellyfish the arms fuse together and sponge-like openings develop on them, through which food is taken in. The ends, however remain free and may have looked like webbed feet.

'A local man found the gas-filled bladder or float of the large stinging jellyfish, the Portuguese man-o-war, *Physalia physalia*, at the end of October on two occasions on the beach at Tacumshin Lake, Co Wexford. The tentacles were gone from both, and the second one was 109mm across. The colour was turquoise tinged with pink."[13]

The Portuguese man-o-war belongs to the same family of coelenterates as the true jellyfish, but they are called hydrozoans, and drift along, carried by the currents, just under the surface of the sea. Each one is a colony of individuals with specific functions: catching food, digesting food, attack, defence, reproduction, suspension in the water and movement. The colony is suspended under a gas-filled float like a balloon, and catches food with the trailing, stinging tentacles. Each tentacle is an individual. The sting can be severe, like a burn, but not fatal.

The velellids are also hydrozoans. 'While walking on Clonea strand, near Dungarvan, in early November, I saw hundreds of soft "animals" on the sand. They were mussel-shaped but firm and jelly-like, with an opaque fin. Five days later they were all gone.'[14] Every year, myriads of by-the-wind-sailors arrive on western and southern strands. These small, oval, bluish discs, with a diagonal sail, are the raft of a jellyfish, *Velella velella*, from which the short tentacles have gone. Like the Portuguese man-o-war they, too, are carried by the currents. The sail is part of the skeleton and is usually mounted north-west to south-east on the raft, which means that it has travelled before the wind from the south-west. We find hundreds of them every year in autumn and early winter, and only on a few has the sail been mounted north-east to south-west. which meant that it had reached us from the north-west.

The variations in the sail's position helps the organism's dispersal through the oceans, and as the by-the-wind-sailors are carried willy-nilly by wind and water, they run a hazard which is just as random as their own movements. If they cross paths with *Janthina*, they will be eaten. *Janthina*, a snail which lives in a beautiful, delicate purple shell, also travels at the whim of the elements, upside down beneath a raft of bubbles it makes itself.

One young reader wanted to know where crabs go in spring. 'I catch lots with barnacles near Kilkee every summer,' he wrote, 'but at Easter I caught none at all.'[15] Many marine animals migrate in winter into deeper water where it is warmer. This a regular practice among edible crabs and prawns and the shore fishes such as blennies that live in summer rock pools. In an extremely cold winter the shore crabs would follow suit. Easter was early in 1989 (March 26th), so they were probably still out there.

If you stand on a weever fish you won't forget it; it is an extremely painful experience. A Dublin correspondent did so while swimming at Brittas Bay, but he was interested to hear about weever fish and if many people have similar incidents.[16] The greater weever is a fish that can be up to 35cm long, and the lesser weever can reach 12cm. They often lie buried in the sand, anywhere from shallow water out to one hundred metres, and leap out to catch crustaceans, sand eels and other small fish. The lesser weever is more likely to be close to the beach. At night they swim freely. The front dorsal fin and the small spines on the gill opening of both fish contain a poisonous sting: weever comes from an old French word for viper. The sting is a nerve poison, and the wound should be allowed to bleed freely and then immersed in very hot water as soon as possible.

Occasionally a beautiful, pink or purple, delicate, spherical shell, with vertical lines of holes, is washed on on the tideline. It is the skeleton or test of a sea urchin which, when living in its natural habitat is covered with spines like a hedgehog. The largest of the Irish urchin species may be the size of a grapefruit, but there are smaller kinds, including one that bores into rock in pools along limestone shores in the west. The tests of the related heart-urchins or sea potatoes feel so delicate in the hand that their arrival ashore in rough weather seems miraculous. 'In the height of the recent gales I found five shells on Kilkee strand. They were almost circular in shape, off-white in colour, very fragile and surprisingly intact. One had short, brown spines on part of its back. Almost two inches in diameter, they had a furrow down their back and a stitch-like effect on the shell.'[17] When heart-urchins are alive they are covered with furry-looking, brownish spines. They are found around all European shores and live in the sand from the lower shore to sea depths of up to two hundred metres.

The egg capsules of fish are among the tideline's more intriguing objects. 'I found a large mermaid's purse on Dunmoran strand. We often find little ones but never one as big as this [life-size drawing of capsule 13 centimetres long was enclosed]. Did it come from a basking shark?'[18] Basking sharks give birth viviparously, that is to live offspring and not eggs enclosed in a capsule. If this egg capsule had four tendrils, it belonged to the greater spotted dogfish. If it had four points, it was the egg capsule of the common skate. The latter is often covered with long sticky hairs.

Another egg capsule yielded a surprise. 'My seven-year-old grandson found two "mermaid's purses", one the usual leathery kind, the other soft and gelatinous, and evidently washed up by the last tide. Imagine our joy on opening the latter to find, not a frog-spawn-like substance, but a miniature skate, 3cm across, and with a tail more than twice as long. At what stage in gestation is this sac ejected, and does the adult skate lay more than one? And, equally perplexing to a small boy, how does the baby get out?'[19] The egg capsules of the thornback ray, one of the commonest on western and southern coasts, are laid in inshore waters in winter shortly after copulation with the male; they are, therefore, often thrown up on the beach. The embryos take about five months to hatch, and the young fish then push their way out.

Seeds from the tropical West Indian vine, *Entada gigas,* journey frequently to our shores. A Belfast visitor found one on the Inishowen Peninsula.[20] These dark-brown, sometimes almost heart-shaped 'beans', measuring three to six centimetres in diameter, are generally found only on the western and southern coasts; we have a modest collection. In earlier times mothers gave them to the babies as teething rings. 'Horse-eye' beans, *Mucuna sloanei* and the grey, acorn-like 'nickar nut', *Caesalpinia bonduc*, are two more of the smaller tropical drift fruits that cross the Atlantic with the Gulf Stream. And there is the occasional coconut, or something even bigger:

'A visitor to the Maritime Museum in Dun Laoghaire brought in an object for identification. It was vegetable, a hemisphere, 46cm in diameter, with leathery, macular skin, concentric rings and a hollow for a nut or kernel. A semi-circular cut across the flesh suggests that this drupe may have been used as a boat fender. It was washed up on Clonpriest Island west of Youghal.'[21] It was the husk of the *coco de mer*, the world's largest seed, up to 50cm, from a palm tree that grows in the Seychelles. In former times, before the palm was discovered, this nut was thought to come from the sea, as it was always found floating, hence the name.

Snorkellers and divers are the only people who can really observe sea fish in their natural medium, and as global warming influences sea temperature and circulation, they are watchful for fish species moving out of their usual latitudes. 'While diving in the Lough Hyne Marine Reserve, near Baltimore, Co Cork, last August, we encountered over a dozen trigger fish swimming within two metres of the surface. Apparently they are visitors to Lough Hyne during warm summers, but they die due to the colder water from October onwards. Their blue hue and lighter coloured thick lips make an exciting visual contrast to the more common fish around our coast.'[22]

A Clare correspondent sent a drawing of a fish found in a lobster pot which had been set in ten fathoms of water three miles north-east of Loop Head, about half-a-mile offshore. 'It was a vertical flat fish and weighed about a pound. The body was grey with shaded areas, nine-and-half inches long by six-and-a-half inches high, and one-and-a-quarter inches wide. It had a brownish coloured spur two-and-a-half inches high on top of its head and thick lips. It was released alive and well.'[23]

This, too, was a trigger fish, *Balistes carolinesis*, whose blue sheen is more visible in the water than out of it. The spur is the first spine of the first dorsal fin which is triggered and locked into an upright position in order to wedge the fish in a crevice, hence the name. It is a common fish around the Azores and Canary Islands and used to be rare in Irish waters. By 1985, however, it appeared to have become a regular summer and autumn visitor.   A recent study[24] suggests that global warming or oceanographic change may be the cause, and it seems likely that when sea temperatures around Ireland fall below critical levels, usually in October, the trigger fish become disoriented, die and are washed ashore.

Freshwater fish have made very few appearances in *Eye on Nature*, but one deserved a mention. 'I was fishing off a bridge on the Slaney about three miles above Baltinglass in the last week in May, when I disturbed a salmon which showed that odd hungry manner that salmon display. It was black as your hat, and I reckon about twelve to fifteen pounds in weight. I have fished this spot for twenty years and have only seen small, brown trout. The obstacles a fish that size had to negotiate in mere inches of water made me think it must have had some helicopter assistance.'[25] The salmon must have come up in a flood to spawn and got stranded.

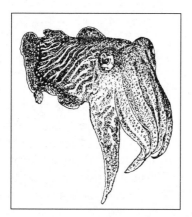
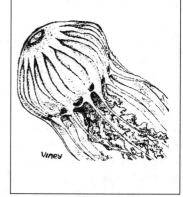

SIXTEEN

LONG LIVE THE WEEDS

There is no better way to start this chapter on plants than with the national emblem, the shamrock. Those of us who are quite sure that we know a shamrock when we see it will be surprised to learn that a controversy exists between botanists and social historians on what exactly *is* a shamrock. One expert put his cards on the table in one of the first columns of *Eye on Nature.*

'Lately I spied in a hedgerow a flowering plant of wood sorrel, *Oxalis acetosella,* sometimes referred to as the true shamrock which brought me to ponder that the shamrock has no botanical recognition. There are many plants adorning lapels on St Patrick's Day, masquerading as the national emblem. Various members of the clover family are to be seen in abundance. One of the family, the lesser yellow trefoil, *Trifolium campestre,* is among the better recognised claimants. It is certainly a better withstander of our climate. The wood sorrel, although by far the more desirable plant, is not frost-hardy; the lovely mat of white, campanulate flowers can succumb to even comparatively mild frosts. It obviously seeks woodland protection for survival. In the times that St Patrick was around, woodland would have abounded, and wood sorrel too.'[1]

There is even further confusion when the various books on flora are consulted: English and Irish botanists do not always agree on the common names of the many clovers that grow in these islands. However the *Census Catalogue of the Flora of Ireland* gives shamrock as a common name for the clover family, and notes that the immature plants of *Trifolium dubium,* yellow clover, *Trifolium repens,* white clover, and *Medicago lupulina,* black medick which is almost indistinguishable before flowering from yellow clover, are most commonly worn as shamrock. All of these are prostrate plants, and a white mark is absent from the leaves of two of them; this is the defining authentication in our locality for 'proper' shamrock.

Some other correspondents remembered another use for wood sorrel. 'A Donegal reader recently recalled the childhood delights of eating various autumnal fruits and berries and also a sour-tasting plant she called "suggies".[2] We also ate this where I was brought up in Down, as doubtless did children all over the country. The plant is wood sorrel, *Oxalis acetocella,* and "suggies" appears to be a form of the Irish name *samhadh coille.* We called it "sour sabs" although some people reserved that name for a related edible plant, common sorrel or sour dock. Wood sorrel is no doubt the "shamrock" or *seamair* which commentators on the Great Famine observed the Irish to eat. I have just seen a rave review of a gourmet sorrel soup served up to a notoriously fastidious lady journalist on some prestigious occasion. Times change.'[3]

Many of the letters about wild flowers extolled their beauty in certain locations. 'Yesterday I walked across Aillwee Mountain from Ballyvaughan to Ballymahon. The top of the mountain is covered with primroses and violets - beautiful!'[4] And down in Kerry: 'I've always associated bluebells with childhood and May altars. A couple of weeks ago while cycling around Muckross, I noticed that Killarney Woods had unfurled their stunning carpets of blue earlier this year. Perhaps one day a romantic poet will visit Killarney in late April and do for the azure beauty of our bluebells what Wordsworth has done for the daffodils.'[5] Gerald Manley Hopkins would have been happy to oblige. He relished 'a juicy and jostling shock/of bluebells sheaved in May'. But in gathering them, don't tread on the leaves: it's trampling not picking that harms them.

Others observed the unseasonable arrival of some flowers in certain years: primroses at Christmas in 1991,[6] and in November in 1995.[7] Unseasonably mild weather in that same month in 1995 upset the natural rhythm of our primroses too, and of their cultivated cousins, the primulas. And in October in Co Leitrim, blossoms appeared on apple trees while they were still in fruit.[8]

The exceptional summer of 1989 caused fuchsia of the hedgerow variety to bear fruit in a Blackrock garden. 'It is heavily laden with fruit, berries about three-quarters of an inch long and a quarter-inch in diameter. The skin is smooth and the colour of an aubergine, and the pulp is juicy and full of tiny seeds. Despite being a keen plant observer, I have never seen a fruiting fuchsia before.'[9] The records say that *Fuchsia magellanica, var, riccartonii,* which is the hedge variety commonly planted in Ireland, hardly ever sets seed or spreads into the wild. It was hybridised at Riccarton in Scotland in 1830 from the South American shrub, and its extraordinary vigour when planted from slips continues its expansion in gardens and at waysides on our moister, frost-free coasts.

Even at the beginning of 1989, plants were blooming in the hedgerows earlier than usual. 'This morning, February 19th, I went for a walk along a narrow country road between Portroe and Garrykennedy. To my amazement I saw bush vetch in full flower. Surely this must be extraordinarily early especially as we are very exposed at five hundred feet above Lough Derg and get every wind that blows.'[10] Bush vetch is not usually due out until April.

Like albinism in birds, the aberrations of flower colour catch the eye. 'Along an unused railway line here in Fenit, there is a large growth of foxgloves for about a quarter of a mile. The flowers are of the usual purplish-red colour except for four stalks together on which the flowers are white.'[11] Another reader saw a similar phenomenon in the woods outside Dungarvan, 'a single, snow-white foxglove surrounded by the usual purple ones'.[12] Colour variations in flowering plants are mainly controlled genetically, and even slight variations in shade may indicate different genetic composition. The foxglove is one of the many wild plants which produce white-flowered varieties. Others are sweet violets, red valerian and heather.

'I was admiring the primroses in the side of a ditch when, to my surprise, I noticed a clump of purple flowers. Is this unusual?'[13] Britain has a very lovely pink-flowered primula with a yellow eye, the bird's eye primrose; and the Scottish primrose has purple flowers with a yellow eye, but is only found in the north of Scotland. Purple forms of garden polyanthus sometimes escape to ditches.

The disappearance of wild flowers over large areas, due to changes in farming methods, is generating more and more concern. 'I grew up in England where fifty years ago, we'd see buttercups and daisies everywhere. In 1947 I went to South Africa, where again there were plenty. Nowhere can I see any buttercups and daisies in Ireland now. Surely they were here in the past? Has some strange disease hit them?'[14] Buttercups are usually found nowadays only in old, permanent pastures and 'unreclaimed' moist meadows. Most fields today have been 'improved' by ploughing and reseeding with a monoculture crop of Italian rye grass. Chemical fertiliser, and sometimes selective herbicides, promote the growth of rye grass for silage and suppress all wild flowers.

Some people are prepared to take a lot of trouble to conserve a particular stand of a threatened plant. 'On a patch of ground at a school near my home, there are several thriving stands of cowslips, the only ones I know for miles around. When I saw the school cutting the grass early this year, I feared for my army of "bunch of keys" flower heads, which towered above the daisies. I went to see the school principal and got a reprieve, halting the decapitation until the end of May, when seed heads would be formed. Hopefully next year there will be double the number of cowslips.'[15]

Another reader, who had been visiting Derry on holidays, wrote from Wales to try to get some authority interested in the preservation of yellow bartsia growing on 'an undeveloped acre of wettish ground' in the Hazelbank area of Derry.[16] Yellow bartsia is relatively scarce but is found in a few places in the west and in Cork and Kerry, and also in Cornwall. Its yellow spire of blossom may reach 45 cm high.

Another uncommon native plant caught the eye of a returned emigrant. 'The three years, 1991-93, have given us a fine show of broomrape, particularly the greater broomrape, growing as it should, two feet tall among a mass of broom. I don't know how common it is in this country but it reminded me of the giant up to six feet broomrape which grows in the salt bush of Saudi Arabia.'[17] Greater broomrape, with its dramatic spikes of rank-smelling flowers, is a parasite on the roots of broom or gorse and grows only in the south-east. As furzy heath is cleared, it seems fated to decline.

The plants which parts of the west of Ireland share with the Iberian peninsula, some heathers, in particular, have posed some difficult questions about their origins. 'The Irish heath is in full flower in March and April. The only place I have seen it is on Claggan Mountain overlooking Bellacragher Bay, near Mulranny in Co Mayo. The mountainside is covered with it. My flower book calls it rare.'[18] The tall and shrubby Irish heath, sometimes called Mediterranean heather, *Erica erigena/mediterranea,* is only found on the coast of Mayo, in several places from Erris Head to Killary Harbour, and in some places in west Galway. It is called Mediterranean heather because it grows also in Spain and Portugal, and western France. After long controversy about the chances of its natural distribution from the south, the most recent research supports the idea that it arrived with early trade or pilgrimage.

Some orchids are notorious for appearing by the thousand in some years and scarcely at all in others. They take years to reach maturity and then spend all their energies on flowering and making prolific quantities of infinitesimal seed. The bee orchid, which grows in dune and limestone pastures and on dry banks is one of these. A group of about ten was reported to *Eye on Nature* from the grass verge of the car park at Shannon airport in 1988.[19] It would be a miracle if they survived 'maintenance' since then. In 1997 we saw them by the score on a limestone knoll in the Turraun Nature Reserve, created from cutaway bog at Lough Boora in Co Offaly.

Those who care about the conservation of our native wild flowers also worry about the importation of wildflower and wild grass seed from outside the country. 'Like a lot of people I am concerned about the wholesale destruction of hedgerows, wild flowers, meadows, marshlands and woodlands. In the school in which I teach, as a contribution to conservation and an educational area for the young, we have created a meadow, a woodland edge with oak, hazel, holly, honeysuckle and rowan, a native hedgerow, a mini-marsh, a tree nursery, a cornfield meadow, a willow grove, bird tables, nest boxes and so on.

'We are concerned, however that a lot of the wildflower and meadow grass seeds had to be imported from England, as they are not available commercially in Ireland. Even though the school is in the inner city of Dublin, we are worried in case these mixtures will have an adverse effect on native flowers and grasses which we also have in abundance in the garden. What about the situation out in the country where a lot of people are sowing imported wild flowers, and when these cross with native species, will the genetic make-up of the latter be affected? Or, are an English cowslip, for example, and an Irish cowslip the same?[20]

Patrick Madden and his pupils created a remarkable wildlife garden in the grounds of Scoil Treasa, Donore Avenue, in inner city Dublin. The garden was started in 1985 and flourishes today as a prototype of a school wildlife garden. An area of about four hundred square metres contains all the above wild habitats, encouraging the wild life, particularly the birds and insects, that are part of a balanced ecosystem. His blueprint for a school wildlife garden, *Go Wild at School*,[21] is a model of 'How To' books, giving detailed instructions which are based on real experience. For some years now, fortunately, Irish wildflower seed has been commercially available,[22] so the problem of genetic interference has receded.

So conditioned are we to think of some wildflowers as 'weeds' that we grudge them any place at all in the countryside. 'When climbing near Mullaghmore, Co Clare, I was horrified to see ragwort growing in the crevices of the rocks with beautiful Burren flora. I envisaged it spreading to other areas and was tempted to pull the weeds up and carry them away for burning elsewhere. But my companion stressed that we should not pull anything growing in this area.'[23] Ragwort is a common wildflower all over the country, and is listed among the notable flowers of the Burren in Gordon D'Arcy's *The Natural History of the Burren*. It has a bad name because it is poisonous to animals when cut and wilted and had been legally termed a 'noxious weed' for that reason.

A more seriously poisonous plant made a surprise appearance in Tipperary. 'It just appeared in my son's front lawn, and we have identified it as a thornapple. He dug a patch and sowed runner beans and sweet peas right in front of the house where the grass had been probably undisturbed for many years. There are a great many of them and we learn that they are poisonous. There are animals and small children in the place, so we would like to know which parts are poisonous and how it comes to be here.'[24] Thornapple, *Datura stramonium*, belongs to the nightshade family and the whole plant is poisonous. When the ground was cultivated, seeds that had lain dormant, for who knows how long, were stirred to germinate: sometimes, large colonies grow up in this way among root crops near the southern coasts. It makes a statuesque plant and the flowers and fruit are attractive, but it should not be left where it might cause danger to animals or people.

Sometimes stirring up the soil's seed-bank can bring an 'extinct' wildflower to life again. Among plants eradicated as weeds from modern cereal farming, both by seed-cleaning and selective herbicides, has been the beautiful blue cornflower. In the late 1980s, it was thought to have been extinct in Ireland for decades, but then just two plants were rediscovered growing in a patch of rye on Inis Mor, largest of the Aran Islands. In the years that followed, a handful of records trickled in to the Wildlife Service, just one or two plants each time and mostly from the disturbed soil at roadsides; only one report, of eighteen plants in a crop of corn in Co Wexford, found the cornflower in its true habitat. In 1997, two more reports reached *Eye on Nature*: one of a clump of plants (bravely photographed) in the centre strip of a new stretch of dual-carriageway near Galway,[25] the other of a few cornflowers blooming at the edge of a grain crop on a farm at Athy, Co Kildare.[26] So the species may be transient and marginalised, but still some way from extinction.

Among our beautiful but invasive aliens, *Rhododendron ponticum* has been the most seriously ecologically harmful, choking off the understorey in the precious oakwoods of Kerry, Donegal and elsewhere. Compared with that, the recent surge in the spread of Japanese knotweed, *Reynoutria japonica*, may seem a minor phenomenon. The shrub was introduced to Britain by gardeners in the nineteenth century, and now regarded as that island's most pernicious weed. Its rapid spread in western Ireland, particularly along roadsides, may be connected simply with the rise in traffic. A Roundstone correspondent wrote that it had become a terrible weed in the area around the town, even growing up through the tarmac of the harbour quay. 'Around here they call it The Curse, because once it gets into your garden, that's it!'[27] And from Co Roscommon: 'I am fighting a losing battle with a shrub which could be a weed, although the profusion of blossom compensates. It is a fierce underground traveller and produces hollow, reddish stalks about seven feet high. The blossom is light and frilly, greenish-white, and the leaves are pointed at the ends'.[28] Japanese knotweed is a perennial plant, making stubborn thickets, but will eventually yield to repeated sprays of glyphosate herbicide.

School buses deprive children of the pleasures of berry-eating along the road on their way to and from school; a regret expressed by a Donegal correspondent. 'On the way home from school in September in the 1930s, we spent hours eating blackberries and picking bilberries which grew on a little hillock close to the road. The wild raspberries were scarcer and it was a case of first come first served. We were often so immersed in our feasting that our school bags were forgotten, but we missed nothing of nature as we walked to school.'[29]

Fraughans or bilberries were plentiful then but are found now only in

tiny pockets in a few places; they have been overgrazed by sheep. A
Limerick reader found dewberries in the sand dunes at Ballybunion. Like
the bilberry they are also rare, but occupy a different habitat: they grow
on sandy and stony places in the south and south-west. 'A local man told
us they were "frauchans" but we knew they weren't. Only some had a few
large segments, and most resembled the raspberry or blackberry in size,
although completely unlike either in taste, with its violet bloom the
dewberry looks beautiful growing in the sand dunes.'[30]

Eye on Nature received one strange berry for identification,[31] it came
from a potato plant. These berries form in occasional years from the
flowers and are poisonous. They contain the seeds of the potato plant, but
normal propagation of potatoes is carried out, as we know, by means of
tubers.

Intensive farming has replaced a dozen or more native grasses in the
meadows of the countryside with the one that responds best to fertiliser -
rye grass. People who take more than a mere casual interest in wildflowers
quickly come to appreciate the beauty and variety of the grasses, the
Graminae, and their place in the island flora. Along with the old fodder
grasses, such as timothy and fescue, were those in the families from which
our modern cereals were bred. A Dublin reader sent in a flowering head
of what he thought might be bristle oat but which had the appearance of
a thin ear of barley. It grew freely, he said near his vegetable patch.[32] It
was, indeed, wild or wall barley, which is common in Britain but found in
Ireland mainly on waste ground around Dublin. The bristle oat lacks the
beard that protects the seeds of the wall barley, and resembles a spike of
ordinary oats; it was a cultivated grain grown in times past, on land too
poor for ordinary oats.

Oats had a place in the mythology of tree-planting according to one
correspondent: 'When planting a tree, as a gift, in the garden of a friend,
he remarked that when he was a child in Co Sligo, his father, a farmer,
when planting a tree would always throw in a fistful of oats, claiming that
it helped to establish the roots. We theorised that perhaps the germinating
oats produced a growth factor, perhaps a hormone or an enzyme, which
was then shared with the sapling. Another friend suggested that perhaps
the oats attracted worms to condition the soil.'[33] Willows produce a
growth promoter; the water in which willow twigs are soaked will help to
root the slips of other plants. Perhaps oats provide a similar substance, or

maybe they turn into a rich compost.

Most people accept trees as just being there, unless they do something out of the ordinary. 'I have ten three-year-old oak seedlings which I grew myself. They are only about twelve inches or less in height, but they have produced about thirty acorns. Since they are growing where I buried a lot of wood ash, I wondered was this the cause of the early reproductive cycle?'[34] This was certainly far too young for oaks to produce acorns. Sometimes, plants flower and fruit early in their lives to ensure reproduction if they are stressed in some way, from drought, say or being planted too close together; but that would not apply to three-year-old oak seedlings. Perhaps the correspondent mistook the galls of the gall wasp for acorns, which they can casually resemble.

A beech tree in full leaf in December through to February perplexed a Dublin reader. 'The tree was about fifteen feet high and the leaves had a more wavy edge than the ordinary beech.'[35]   It was an evergreen, Dombey's southern beech, which is usually found in gardens. One at Mount Ussher is twenty-seven metres tall.

There are good and bad years for the production of beech mast, and many readers reported that 1988 and 1991 were good years. (The word 'mast' comes from the Scandinavian 'mat' meaning food.) Scarce years usually follow on the good years, because heavy seed-bearing exhausts the reserves of many trees, and they need a year or two to recover. As the flower buds which eventually form the seeds are set the previous year, heavy crops tend to occur in four-year cycles, particularly in beeches and oaks. 'We live on the edge of St Anne's woods, and we have noticed, for the first time in forty years, that the holm oak overhanging the footpath opposite our house has shed thousands of acorns.'[36] Weather conditions of all sorts, such as good growing conditions in spring and summer, or frost or storms in spring, will also affect crop size.

Non-native trees, such as sweet chestnuts, require special conditions and 1991 was a good year for them. 'I have always understood that the sweet (Spanish) chestnut, native to southern Europe, only produced fruit here in especially good summers. Imaging my pleasure at finding a carpet of the white, open fruit, containing two or three nuts, strewn beneath a fine specimen in Lough Key Forest Park recently. Most of the nuts were "gluggers" but I saved some whole ones and intend to grow them.'[37]

The nuts of sweet chestnut will ripen here in a good summer, but usually only one or two nuts develop in each cluster. The tree is relatively easy to grow but not in chalk or limestone. We have grown one at Thallabawn in relatively poor soil.

'The public house in Culdaff is an ideal place to visit when one has a query. It is a matter of listen and learn. The subjects can range from botany and biology to political affairs, national and international. During the week I posed one question. Sycamore, mountain ash and elder reproduce by the mere dropping of their respective seeds here and there at random. However, sitka spruce and *pinus contorta* do not reproduce without special planting. Why, I asked the experts. No one, I regret to say had an answer. However, not to be beaten, they said why not ask *Eye on Nature*.'[38]

Even though they are foreign conifers, both sitka spruce and *pinus contorta* (lodge pole pine) set viable seed in Ireland, and will produce 'wild' seedlings in the right conditions. But sitka planted in close plantations spends its energies on growing and keeping its place in the rising leaf canopy, so it usually postpones flowering until fairly late in life. Self-sown seedlings may not be seen until a sitka stand is clear-felled at fifty or sixty years old, when quite a luxuriant carpet of seedlings may spring up in the light. Lodge pole pine, on the other hand, with a more open growth, flowers very early in life and seedlings can be found beside quite young plantations, particularly on the bare mineral soil along forest roads; they would not normally germinate in the litter of the forest floor.

Dutch elm disease decimated the elms of Europe and North America over recent decades; they died in their millions (four and a half million in Britain by 1974), leaving gaps in woods and hedgerows. Irish elms did not escape, but elms do not figure so largely in Irish woodland; they are found mainly on private estates and in hedgerows. 'I have a small wood, and I lost about forty mature trees to Dutch elm disease. Since then I have noticed elm suckers growing from the roots and stumps of the old trees; and I found a couple of quite large, new trees, one of which is about eighteen feet high and apparently healthy. Is there any evidence that the disease has ceased to affect us, perhaps for lack of elms? Can diseased tree be recognised at an early stage by some sign?'[39]

Dutch elm disease is cause by the fungus *Ceratocystis ulmi*, the spores of which are carried by elm bark beetles from dead or dying elms to healthy trees. The beetles feed on the bark of the tree in the crotches of branches where they introduce the spores. The first signs are patches of yellowing leaves in the crown of the tree in summer, and wilting twigs later. The disease can be controlled by destroying the beetles on dead and dying trees, and felling diseased trees to destroy the bark.

Widespread and common, hawthorn is the best known tree of our hedgerows. As it tends to be regularly clipped it is more usually a bush than the impressive tree it can become; but its blossoms in May are always an arresting sight. 'This has been a remarkable year for blossom of all sorts, but I noticed, as did some of my friends, that there was much more pink of various shades on the hawthorns. I also noticed that hawthorns that were pink a few years ago have not been so since. Is it known what causes pinkness?'[40]

Most flower colour is genetically controlled, and mutations within Ireland's hawthorns throw up occasional pink forms, but their colour is constant from year to year. White hawthorn blossom can take on a pinkness as they decay, perhaps these pink blossoms were observed in June or later as they came to the end of their blooming.

Hawthorn figures in Irish myth, magic and legend, and out of that body of lore a Westport reader contributed a little known story. 'A French historian, Gerard Aubertin, who frequently visits Westport, wrote in our local, historical journal about the traditional association of St Patrick with a small village near Tours. It appears that, in addition to a small church dedicated to our patron saint, there is, in the locality, a hawthorn bush which flowers at Christmas. There is a similar tradition regarding St Patrick and Glastonbury in England, where also, apparently, there is a thorn bush which flowers at Christmas; it was supposed to have been planted by Joseph of Arimathea. Last year on St Stephen's Day I drove to a number of sites associated with St Patrick in Mayo and Roscommon, but not a flower was to be seen anywhere.'[41]

The Glastonbury thorn is botanically *Crategus monogyna var praecox* , a variety of the common hawthorn which puts out leaves and flowers in winter and again in May. The original tree was supposed to have grown from Joseph's stick when he stuck it in the ground on Wearyall Hill, in Glastonbury, on his arrival in Britain in 63AD. Cuttings planted at Glastonbury down the centuries have kept the legend of the tree alive to the present day. The tree planted in 1900 died in 1991, but three younger trees grow nearby. There is no record of it growing wild in Ireland, but it can be found in the Kennedy Memorial Park at New Ross, Co Wexford, where it is listed as *Crataegus monogyna var biflora.*

Another wayside bush, the elder, is also rich in folklore. 'We have some old elders in our garden. Though there are other varieties of trees, our own cats as well as strange cats make a beeline for one special elder where they have uncovered part of it root. The rub their heads and shoulders at this root as if there were some "medicine" in it. Kittens seem to know it by instinct. If we cover that part up they immediately dig it up again.'[42] The folklore of the elder is rich in witches but makes no mention of cats. However, the same behaviour is aroused in cats by the herbaceous border plant, *Nepeta* or catmint, which has an aromatic odour which cats love. Elder root contains a volatile oil which may well have an exciting odour that the cats have discovered. Elder has also many uses in herbal medicine.

Beyond the columns of *Eye on Nature*, a controversy exists around the subject of ivy, and it also surfaced here. 'Many of our native trees throughout the country are hosting what I would call dangerous growths of ivy, stifling their growth, preventing development and in many cases acting as a wind sail in storms. Cutting out or curtailment of ivy is now rarely observed. If every schoolboy tackled the ivy on ten native trees before the summer break, then a start would have been made.'[43] Recently an eminent person (in another discipline) published a book which declared war in strong terms on ivy.[44] There is expert opinion which holds that ivy only overgrows weak and dying trees. It can co-exist with a strong tree, as noted by Dr Oliver Rackham in his *History of the Countryside:* 'On an island in a boggy lough in Co Offaly is an extraordinary wood of great ancient oaks, hung with ancient ivies, one ivy trunk is thicker than a fat man...' It is arguable that, in the distinctive climate of Ireland, ivy has achieved an exuberance it is denied further east, and that the bulk of an ivy tod in the crown of a tree does sometimes inhibit its final growth or lead to its premature loss in high winds. But this, if true, is part of a natural ecosystem: to interfere with it is 'gardening'. In ivy's favour it must be said that it provides food and shelter throughout the year to many birds and insects, and does not feed on the tree.

Dislike, however, exists widely. 'Last December I cut near the ground strong growths of ivy from two adjacent ash trees. After three months one ivy completely died away, but the other has remained green and healthy. What can have kept the second ivy alive for twelve months, cut off, as it is, from its roots, and deriving no sustenance from its host?'[45] The ivy's adhesive fibres draw no sustenance from the tree. But where they encounter a deep crevice filled with humus, or a pocket of soil, these fibres will then become true roots and feed on it. The second ash may have harboured some secret food supply of that kind.

'On one of my silver birches, a twenty-year-old, not a very strong tree, five or six growths have formed. At first sight they look like crow's nests, but on examining one I found it made of interlaced, small branch work, circular in shape and perhaps eight to nine inches in diameter. They appear to be growths on the tree.'[46] These clusters of twigs are called witch's broom and they affect birches, conifers and cherry. They can be caused by either a fungus, a virus or damage to the bud. They do no harm to the tree, but they can be cut off if considered unsightly; the wound should be painted to avoid infection. In a similar situation a hawthorn would grow a gall around an injured area.

If *Eye on Nature* appeared in a newspaper in Continental Europe, observations and queries about edible fungi would certainly loom large among the letters, but the Irish involvement with the wide range of mushrooms is timid, to say the least. 'My Italian husband is an enthusiastic mycologist who, in his own country, brings home basketfuls of *boletus, cantharellus, clitocybes, hygrophorus, russula, tricholoma,* etc. Do these mushrooms grow in Ireland? When I ask friends and acquaintances in Dublin they refer me to field mushrooms, and refer to all others as poisonous. Does Ireland have its edible varieties of mushrooms as well as their poisonous counterparts, like the delicious *Amanita caesarea* and the deadly poisonous *Amanita phalloides*? Or do our woods and forests only yield the 'fairy toadstools' all children are warned never to touch?'[47]

Boletus edulis, the penny bun or cep, highly appreciated by Continental cooks, is found in woodlands in Ireland, as are *cantharellus*, the Chanterelle, several species of *clitocybes, hygrophorus* and *russula* and also blewitts. *Amanita caesarea*, also known as Caesar's or royal mushroom, belongs to warmer woods, mostly south of the English Channel. However, the poisonous *Amanita phalloides*, the death cap and *Amanita muscaria*, fly agaric, are to be found in Ireland and, of course, must be left strictly alone.

There are others that rarely get mentioned. 'On Rathfarnham golf course, on March 30th, I came upon about six well-developed field mushrooms which seemed quite authentic and edible. I took them home,

cooked them, for safety, took only one for a start. It was quite delicious.
But surely it is very unusual to be picking field mushrooms in March.'[48]
The ordinary field mushroom, *Agaricus campestris*, doesn't appear until
July;   but the excellent St George's mushroom, *Calocybe gambosum*,
appears in spring, usually in April, and also grows on open grassland,
especially on limey soils. It has a distinctive, mealy smell, and white - not
pinky-brown - gills. It would not be hard to mistake it for a large field
mushroom. We have eaten and enjoyed St George's but would shun any
mushroom we weren't absolutely sure about. Of the deadly, white-gilled
Amanita even one can be too many.

'In the first week in November, while on a day shooting pheasant in
Williamstown, Co Westmeath, I came across what I thought was a puffball
growing under a mature ash tree. I was amazed at the size of it. It
measured about fourteen inches from ground to top, and a good sixteen
inches from side to side. I estimated the weight to be five or six pounds.'[49]
The giant puffball, *Langermannia gigantica*, reaches forty to fifty
centimetres or more and weighs several kilograms; this one was forty
centimetres. When it was fresh, before the spores matured, it could have
weighed more than ten kilograms.

Giant puffballs are a separate species, not the small, common puffball
writ large. These grow in the same place every year, sometimes in rings,
on rich soil, and are good to eat when the flesh is young and white. Later
it turns yellow, and finally brown.

Many people have noticed that field mushrooms tend to grow in a ring,
which is the way the colony develops if conditions are right, but one
observer also noticed another effect. 'A ring of dark green grass with
mushrooms in it has appeared in our lawn. This has never happened
before in the fourteen years we have lived here. What causes it, fairies
apart?'[50]   Mushrooms reproduce vegetatively as well as by dispersal of
spores. The fungus produces fruiting bodies, the mushrooms, only in
years when conditions are favourable; but it continues to spread under the
ground, and a circle is the shape the spreading mycelia form. The grass is
a darker colour on the ring because mushrooms grow by breaking down
material in the soil, releasing nutrients such as nitrogen.

SEVENTEEN

OVER THE RAINBOW

Newcomers to the countryside see natural phenomena with a freshness that often surprises. 'On a morning walk up our boreen on December 5th we saw a complete rainbow in the field alongside us, We are relatively new to living in Ireland and to us it was a remarkable sight so close to us. However on January 17th we saw an even more remarkable sight. It was a misty morning and the sun was just shining through. In virtually the same place there was a bright, white arc composed of the mist itself. The top of the arc was less distinct than either of its ends. How unusual is this phenomenon?'[1] The white arc was caused by the refraction and reflection of the sun's rays in ice crystals in the mist. It is not a commonly observed phenomenon because it requires a certain degree of mist, sun behind it, and, of course, an observer at the right angle.

Rainbows are always special, but sometimes there are special rainbows. 'I was looking north-east from Roundstone towards Cashel Hill, a couple of miles away, when I saw a rainbow with spokes. The setting sun was shining through a small rent in the cloud bank behind me, and the rainbow seemed to centre upon the top of the hill. The hill itself behind it was brilliantly illuminated, and streaks of brightness and darkness seemed to be radiating from the hill, or just behind, out from the rainbow.

'After much puzzling, I understood the appearance as follows: The light and dark "rays" we see fanning out from the edges of clouds covering the sun are the projections of their shadows into moisture-filled air, and of course they are, in fact, parallel; if they continued overhead they would appear to converge on a spot opposite to the sun. In this case the shadows were being formed in aerial moisture north-east of me, where the rainbow was also being formed, so both rainbow and the fan of shadow appeared

153

centred in the same spot. The result was a few spectacular minutes in the endless configuration of the Connemara sky.'[2]

The refraction of the sun's rays through the different manifestations of water, or through the facets of a crystal, is a more prosaic way of explaining the beauty of the rainbow effect in its many different forms. 'I think one of the most fascinating sights I ever saw was when I was swimming in summer on a wild and windy day, with large waves breaking on the shore. The wind blew the tops of the waves back, and for a few seconds tiny little rainbows appeared each time a wave was about to break,[3] Fairies, riding the white horses?

The rainbow occurred on the wave tops in the same way that a rainbow is formed in the sky. The different wavelength components of the sun's rays were refracted through the drops in the sea spray at slightly different angles inside each drop, breaking up the light into its different colours. The sun would have been behind the observer in this case, as it would in the case of a rainbow in the sky.

The Irish language has names for many different winds, fashioned in times when their character, benign or malevolent, really mattered. 'We live right by the sea at Dunmore East, Co Waterford, and when the potato crop was just emerging we were hit by a violent wind which burned the potatoes and other plants, and even weeds in the hedges. What was that wind? It wiped out 90% of our crop.'[4] An ill wind! The one known in the west as *an gaoth ruadh*, the red wind, arrives from the sea in July and burns vegetation with the salt it carries. Strong, dry winds at that time of year would also desiccate foliage, especially young soft growth.

The mirrored image in still water of a lovely scene is the stuff of picture postcards, but its reality is also enchanting. 'In mid-November, while driving past the lower lake in Glendalough I had a most extraordinary experience. I thought the water had gone from the lake, and the crater was lined with trees and bushes right to the bottom. There was no wind and the surface of the water reflected everything.'[5]

The magic of a clear night sky is lost to the millions who live in towns, wrapped in a nimbus of scattered and reflected artificial light. Few people saw the aurora borealis that disturbed one reader's springer spaniel in 1989 (see Chapter 9). Those who live on the north coast of Mayo, and indeed on all the north-west and north coasts, see the aurora regularly, as Ethna did when she lived in Killala. A Co Down correspondent had his own heavenly moment. 'On the night of November 11th, 1989, many sources reported a strange light in the sky. I live in the country, so there are no street lights to dazzle. As I walked down the yard the whole place was illuminated by a bluish-white light which lasted rather longer than a lightning flash. Looking up to the south-west I saw a swiftly-moving streak of bluish-white light with a roundish mass in front. Behind this larger ball came three smaller masses at irregular intervals. Each of the 'lumps' had a blunt tail of more intense bluish-white. Almost as soon as I saw it the sky darkened again.

'The Planetarium in Armagh told me I had been lucky enough to see a spectacular meteor, perhaps as small as a car or as large as a house, which had crossed above the Irish Sea at anything from seventeen to fortymiles above the Earth, and had probably burned itself out in the atmosphere.'[6]

NOTES

REFERENCES

Chapter 1
A Commotion of Crows

1   J M King, Rossanrubble, Newport,
    Co Mayo (21/1/90)
2   Mark Helmore, Burren, Co Clare.
    (13/4/96)
3   Ursula O'Farrell, Booterstown,
    Co Dublin. (4/11/89)
4   Robert A Christie, Greencastle,
    Co Donegal. (2/1/93)
5   Nuala Denniss, Schull, Co Cork.
    (3/2/96)
6   Elizabeth Fitzgerald, Borris,
    Co Carlow. (17/12/94)
7   Frank Newport, Muff, Co Donegal.
    (3/7/93)
8   Patsy Connolly, Ballyvaughan,
    Co Clare. (11/5/91)
9   Martina Sheer, Dunboyne, Co Meath.
    (6/8/95)
10 Wayne Harlow, Streamstown,
    Westport, Co Mayo. (9/10/93)
11 J Roycroft, St Brendan's Drive,
    Dublin, 5. (8/4/89)
12 Val Byrne, Clondalkin. Dublin, 22.
    (28/5/94)
13 Terry Doyle, Dundrum, Dublin, 16.
    (11/11/95)
14 Eithne Scallan, Wexford. (2/2/91)
15 Brendan J Walker, Carlow. (25/2/95)
16 Eugene Loftus, Ballina, Co Mayo.
    (13/4/96)
17 Ulli and Ika Peiler, Ballymote,
    Co Sligo. (13/8/94)
18 P M Close, Larne, Co Antrim.
    (7/12/91)
19 Kenneth Collins, Clonsilla,
    Co Dublin. (May 1995)
20 Kieran Fitzpatrick, Greystones,
    Co Wicklow. (24/3/88)
21 Sean Bean, Maynooth, Co Kildare.
    (22/1/94)

22 Paul Higgins, Longford. (10/8/96)
23 Anne Potterton, Kildalkey, Co Meath.
    (31/3/90)
24 Winifred Power, Douglas Cork.
    (24/6/95)
25 David O'Connor, Woodstown,
    Co Waterford. (12/3/94)
26 Sheila Pim, Westfield, Dublin.
    (4/6/88)
27 Michael McInerney, Kinvara,
    Co Galway. (12/10/96)

Chapter 2
Thrush on a Merry-go-round

1   Mary McKeogh, Kilkenny. (31/5/97)
2   Trish Hyde, Camas Park Stud,
    Cashel, Co Tipperary. (16/4/88)
3   Jim O'Neill, Stillorgan, Co Dublin.
    (10/4/93; 30/4/94)
4   Mike Boggins, Foxford, Co Mayo.
    (8/6/91)
5   Norma Hastings, Glenbeigh,
    Co Kerry. (16/7/88)
6   Margaret Thompson, Shankill,
    Co Dublin. (4/3/95)
7   James Doyle, Carrigloe, Cobh,
    Co Cork. (23/9/89)
8   Seán MacEochaidh, Nás na Riogh,
    Cill Dara. (10/8/91)
9   John J Walsh, Bagenalstown,
    Co Carlow. (22/6/91)
10 Hugh Delaney, Cabinteely,
    Co Dublin. (8/4/89)
11 Nick McAuliffe, Clonmel,
    Co Tipperary. (1/3/97)
12 Miriam Tobias, Ballyroan, Laois.
    (27/4/91)
13 Meriel Murdock, Kilmacanogue,
    Co Wicklow. (20/5/95)
14 B J Walker, Carlow. (11/6/94)
15 Geraldine Leonard, Ballinteer,
    Dublin, 16. (16/2/91)

16   James Dully, Pembroke Rd, Dublin, 4. (25/2/95)

17   Alvie McConnell, Lisnakilly, Limavady, Co Derry. (11/6/88)

18   Harry Bond, Killuran, Enniscorthy, Co Wexford. (10/5/97)

19   Tom Huston, Ballintemple, Cork. (2/9/89)

20   Tom Murray, Raheny, Dublin, 5. (4/6/94)

21   Ray McGinty, Beaumont, Dublin, 9. (22/6/96)

22   Michael Coote, Rathgar, Dublin, 6. (28/1/95)

23   Harold Agnew, Kells, Co Antrim. (5/2/94)

24   Harry Latham, Killiney, Co Dublin. (13/2/93)

25   Noel Byrne, Riverstown, Birr, Co Offaly. (15/1/94)

26   Andrew Trentham, Eyrecourt, Co Galway. (28/3/92)

27   Felicity MacDermot, Monasterden, Co Sligo. (10/2/96)

28   Mrs N Loughlin, Galtrim Road, Bray, Co Wicklow. (4/11/89)

Chapter 3
Table Manners

1   A Taylor, Killakee, Dublin, 16. (2/7/94)

2   Margaret Priey, Sidmonton Road, Bray, Co Wicklow. (18/2/89)

3   Kilian Kelly, Redbarn, Youghal, Co Cork. (15/5/93)

4   Harry Latham, Killiney, Co Dublin. (3/7/93)

5   Leigh Carson, Rathmines, Dublin, 6. (9/3/91)

6   B Landy, Templeogue, Dublin, 16. (16/1/93)

7   Frank Smyth, Sutton, Dublin, 13. (5/9/92)

8   Valerie Wallace, Helen's Bay, Co Down. (15/2/92)

9   Vera McSweeney, Galway. (1/2/97)

10   Lucy S Johnson, Marfield Garden Centre, Cabinteely, Dublin, 18. (21/1/89)

11   Trish Hyde, Camas Park Stud, Cashel, Co Tipperary. (19/4/97)

12   Jim Leonard, Tramore, Co Waterford. (2/1/93)

13   Bernie Norris, Dungarvan, Co Waterford. (9/7/94)

14   M Doyle, Malin Head, Co Donegal. (14/9/91)

15   K Clerkin, Baltinglass, Co Wicklow. (2/7/94)

16   R K Page, Grange Con, Co Wicklow. (4/3/89)

17   Frank Smyth, Sutton, Dublin, 13. (5/9/92).

18   Andrea Martin, St Mary's Road, Dublin, 4. (17/12/94)

19   Eileen Murphy, Abbeyfeale, Co Limerick. (1/3/97)

20   Brian Kennedy, Jamestown Bridge, Co Leitrim. (25/3/95)

Chapter 4
Seasonal Visitors

1   Pádraig Ó Loinsigh, Castlecove, Derrynane, Co Kerry. (16/4/88)

2   Raymond Morgan, Stillorgan, Co Dublin. (11/4/92)

3   Maev Doyle, Clonskeagh, Dublin, 6. (30/7/88)

4   Hugh Sacker, Donard, Co Wicklow. (3/6/95)

5   Pat Mulcahy, Cork. (30/4/88)

6   Geraldine Kyne, Corcullen, Galway. (16/9/95)

7   Gillies MacBain, Cranagh Castle, Templemore, Co Tipperary. (11/8/90)

8   Lucy O'Reilly, Kilcock, Co Kildare. (13/1/90)

9   Eileen Tansley, Tralee, Co Kerry. (6/1/90)

10   Arthur Moore, Mooresfort, Tipperary. (15/10/94)

11   Niamh Neumann, Newcastle, Co Wicklow. (24/5/95)

12   Gregory Daly, Boyle, Co Roscommon. (27/8/94)

13   Ann Cowie, Blessington, Co Wicklow. (20/8/88)

14   H Melville, Dartry, Dublin, 6. (12/8/89)

15   R McGovern, Sandymount,
     Dublin, 4. (1/9/90)

16   Rev Ignatius Fennessy, Killiney,
     Co Dublin. (4/4/92)

17   Brigid O'Donnell, Culdaff,
     Co Donegal. (23/6/90)

18   Máire Pearson, Dundrum, Dublin,
     16. (17/12/94)

19   James Moran, Athleague,
     Co Roscommon. (7/6/95)

20   Barry Meagher, Ballsbridge, Dublin,
     4. (7/10/95)

21   Charles Acton, Carrickmines, Dublin,
     18. (10/7/93)

22   William MacDougald, Castledermot,
     Co Kildare. (26/8/95)

23   Tony Creedon, Kingswood Heights,
     Tallaght, Dublin, 24. (6/5/89)

24   Peter Jankowski, Stillorgan,
     Co Dublin. (1/6/91)

25   (4/5/96)

26   Una de Breadun, Rossinver,
     Co Leitrim (27/4/91)

27   Terry Carruthers, Killarney, Co Kerry
     (11/5/91)

28   M.P. Sands, Ferrybank, Co Waterford
     (6/9/97)

29   Lisa Mongey (aged 8), Tramore,
     Co Waterford. (24/4/93)

30   Bernie Bourke, Colmanstown,
     Menlough, Co Galway. (18/5/96)

31   John Jennings, Cross, Claremorris,
     Co Mayo. (30/10/93)

32   M Carroll, Sandymount, Dublin, 4.
     (9/11/96)

Chapter 5
And a Partridge in a pear tree

1   Herbert J Ahern, Boyle,
     Co Roscommon. (19/11/88)

2   Eugene Kelly, Glenageary, Co Dublin.
     (6/4/91)

3   A C Anderson, Churchtown, Dublin,
     14. (9/3/91).

4   Sr Vianney McLoughlin, Ballinasloe,
     Co Galway. (19/12/92)

5   Michael Van Dessek, Fahan,
     Co Donegal. (30/3/96)

6   (17/6/89)

7   Brian Reynolds, Nire Valley,
     Co Waterford. (12/9/92)

8   J F Carmody, Kilrush, Co Clare.
     (30/8/97)

9   Judith Hinchkiff, Barnaboy,
     Rossnowlagh, Co Donegal. (14/7/90)

10   David Cabot, Dalkey, Co Dublin.
     (10/6/89)

11   John E Byrne, Downings,
     Co Donegal. (11/3/95)

12   P C Cooney, Carpenterstown,
     Co Westmeath. (5/10/91)

13   Martin Zajac, Killala, Co Mayo.
     (29/10/88)

14   M Grace, Ballycommon, Nenagh,
     Co Tipperary. (16/2/91)

15   Diana Macauley, Blessington,
     Co Wicklow. (4/3/89)

16   Jim Fox, Coursetown, Athy,
     Co Kildare. (10/6/89; 4/11/89)

17   Séan Lysaght, Westport, Co Mayo.
     (3/6/95)

18   Leo Morahan, Kilmurry,
     Crossmolina, Co Mayo. (4/6/94)

19   Eugene O'Callaghan, Knockboy,
     Waterford. (10/9/88)

Chapter 6
Wild Calls in the Sky

1   William McEwan, Wheatfield Road,
     Palmerstown, Dublin, 20. (21/10/89)

2   Morna Hilton, Annascaul, Co Kerry.
     (29/6/91)

3   T P McNamara, Keel, Achill,
     Co Mayo. (24/11/90)

4   Ethel Woolfe, Ranelagh, Dublin, 6.
     (14/5/94)

5   John Kilbracken, Killegar,
     Co Leitrim. (11/3/89)

6   Paddy McClure, Gort-na-Cool,
     Carndonagh, Co Donegal.
     (28/10/89)

7   Tom Murray, Raheny, Dublin, 5.
     (8/10/84)

8   Michael Logan, Phibsboro, Dublin, 7.
     (5/6/93)

9   Michael H Coote, Rathgar, Dublin,
     6. (20/7/96)

10   Jim Sutton, New Ross, Co Wexford.
     (19/9/92)

11 Patrick Harrold, Corwen, Clwyd, North Wales. (20/11/93)

12 Rory Brown, Gowran, Co Kilkenny. (29/10/94)

13 Patrick Druggan, Oughterard, Co Galway. (29/8/92)

14 Robin Harte, Knockmaroon, Chapelizod, Dublin, 20. (27/8/94)

15 James H Casey, Dun Laoghaire, Co Dublin. (2/3/96)

16 Michael Purser, Killiney, Co Dublin. (5/12/92)

17 Denis Coghlan, Blackrock, Co Dublin. (30/4/88)

18 Patrick J Coyle, Laytown, Co Meath. (14/5/88)

19 Martin Byrne, Oranmore, Co Galway. (14/1/95)

20 Ann O'Sullivan, Saleen, Co Cork (??/9/95)

21 Sean Hegarty, Carrowmore, Louisburgh, Co Mayo. (18/12/93)

22 Dermot Hourihane, Monkstown, Co Dublin. (8/2/97)

23 Brenda Morley, Cork & Alice Smyth, Drogheda. (25/3/95)

24 Dermot Edwards, Lismore, Co Waterford. (12/6/93)

25 Mike Flood (aged 9), Clonlara, Co Clare. (24/5/97)

26 Margaret M Sargent, Rathmines, Dublin, 6. (19/1/91)

27 Una O'Sullivan, Rathmines, Dublin, 6. (15/6/96)

28 Tom O'Sullivan, Victoria Square, Rostrevor, Co Down. (8/4/89)

29 A W and J Johnston, Woodford Bridge Essex. (15/5/93)

30 Emma (7) and Ruth (5) Turpin, Percy Place, Dublin, 4. (12/12/92)

31 Frank Turpin, Percy Place, Dublin, 4. (10/8/91)

32 Martin Byrnes, Oranmore, Co Galway. (24/8/91)

33 Mary Zeimbeki, Cloonflush, Tuam, Co Galway. (11/4/92)

34 Norman E Hoey, Landgarve Manor, Crumlin, Co Antrim. (23/5/92)

35 Daphne Sweeney, Loughlinstown, Co Dublin. (21/8/93)

Chapter 7
Birds at the Tide

1 Rodney Devitt, Sandymount, Dublin, 4. (29/4/89)

2 Tim O'Brien, Glenageary, Co Dublin. (13/1/96)

3 Howard Fox, Coursetown, Athy, Co Kildare. (1/4/95)

4 John Cussen, Newcastle West, Co Limerick. (3/3/90)

5 Paddy McClure, Carndonagh, Co Donegal. (28/11/92)

6 John R Roy, Dalkey, Co Dublin. (16/3/96)

7 Veronica McGovern, Rathmines, Dublin, 6. (18/5/96)

8 Joe Ducke, Crannaghbeg, Athlone, Co Westmeath. (19/12/92)

9 Paddy Heraughty, The Mall House, Sligo. (9/9/89)

10 Kevin Gormley, Stillorgan, Co Dublin. (7/4/90)

11 Sean Healy, Caherdaniel, Co Kerry. (3/3/90)

12 John and Joie Myles, Greencastle, Co Donegal. (4/4/92)

13 Brian Scott, Glenarm, Co Antrim. (7/7/90)

14 Dorothea Snoek, Kilmuckridge, Co Wexford. (1/4/95)

15 Rory Brown, Gowran, Co Kilkenny. (29/10/94)

16 Rosemary Rudd, Waterville, Co Kerry. (13/8/88)

17 Dorothea Snoek, Kilmuckridge, Co Wexford. (1/4/95)

Chapter 8
Fearless on the Lawn

1 Tomas O'Toole, Dungloe, Co Donegal. (6/1/90)

2 Les Stocker, The Complete Fox; David Macdonald, *Running with the Fox.*

3 Richard Nairn, Ashford, Co Wicklow. (14/1/89)

4 Claire Fleming, Blackrock, Co Dublin. (15/2/92)

5 Mark Turpin, Pembroke Road, Dublin, 4. (11/1/92)

6   Des Lally, Ballynahinch Castle Hotel, Co Galway. (27/11/93)

7   Eileen O'Brien, Inistioge, Co Kilkenny. (21/1/95)

8   Robert Newell, Ballywaltrim, Bray, Co Wicklow. (24/4/93)

9   Colleen Bresnihan, Ransboro, Co Sligo. (3/8/91)

10   Frank Gallagher, Inchiquin-on-Corrib, Co Galway. (23/10/93)

11   Orla Dunlevy, Ventry, Co Kerry. (8/10/84)

12   Esther M Phelan, Ashford, Co Wicklow. (9/9/89)

13   Marilynn Hearne, Tramore, Co Waterford. (30/6/90)

14   Aine Doyle, Mount Prospect Stud, Rathangan, Co Kildare. (5/5/90)

15   Mark Regan, Cong National School, Co Mayo. (4/12/93)

16   J McCarthy, District Veterinary Officer, Dept of Agriculture, Cork.

17   Gill Bonar, Dunfanaghy, Co Donegal. (7/5/88)

18   Walter Roberts, Dalkey, Co Dublin. (15/1/94)

19   Melissa Deegan, Ballyore Road, Rathfarnham, Dublin, 14. (25/11/89)

20   R Sterling, Nenagh, Co Tipperary. (26/7/97)

21   Roy Kirwan (aged 8), Gorey, Co Wexford. (3/8/91)

22   Joseph A Kelly, Blackrock, Co Dublin. (30/9/95)

23   Kevin Collins, Tuam, Co Galway. (28/1/95)

24   Brian Morwood, Drumcose, Enniskillen, Co Fermanagh. (4/8/90)

25   Gregory Daly, Finsbury Park, London. (3/12/88)

26   John MacNamara, Admiral's Rest, Fanore, Co Clare.

27   Michael F Corbett, Curraghgower House, The Strand, Limerick. (14/1/89)

28   Betty Williams, Coolbawn, Nenagh, Co Tipperary. (24/9/88)

29   J Carmody, Kilrush, Co Clare. (27/6/92)

30   Niall Walsh, Dromahair, Co Leitrim. (16/11/96)

31   Marcus Horan, Clonlara, Co Clare. (14/3/92)

32   Paul Kneafsey, Ballymachugh, Ballycastle, Co Mayo. (31/8/96)

33   Diana Macaulay, Blessington, Co Wicklow. (3/2/90)

34   Anon. (14/9/91)

35   Jonathan Mason, Lusk, Co Dublin. (20/2/91)

36   Brid Cleary, Ballyhaunis, Co Mayo. (24/3/90)

37   Michael D. Coyle, Sandymount, Dublin, 4. (18/2/89)

38   Among them: Henry Williamson's *Tarka the Otter*, Gavin Maxwell's *Ring of Bright Water*, Philip Wayre's *Operation Otter.*

39   Jim Murphy, Monaghan. (13/11/93)

40   Michael Purser, Killiney, Co Dublin. (20/8/94)

41   M McDonald, Navan Road, Dublin, 7. (24/7/93)

42   Rory Brown, Cloghala, Co Kilkenny. (2/4/94)

43   Kevin Gormley, Stillorgan, Co Dublin. (12/8/95)

44   Grace Sheridan, Waterford. (30/4/94)

45   Janet Ashe, Newtownmountkennedy, Co Wicklow. (23/4/94)

Chapter 9
The mouse that ate winkles

1   Michael Sheehan, Hayman's Hill, Youghal, Co Cork. (25/8/90)

2   Victor McAlmont, Norelands, Stonyfort, Co Kilkenny. (4/8/90)

3   M K Page, Grangecon, Co Wicklow. (6/5/89)

4   Pauline Hickie, Terryglass, Co Tipperary. (12/10/91)

5   Anon. (22/4/89)

6   Norma Malcolm, Carrignagaw, Lismore, Co Waterford. (30/12/89)

7   Miriam Tobias, Ballyroan, Co Laois. (27/4/91)

8   Esther O'Mahony, Fenit, Co Kerry. (3/8/91)

9   Bob Newell, Bray, Co Wicklow. (11/5/96)

10   Brian McFerran, Holywood,
      Co Down. (17/9/94).

11   Eamon McGinn, Sutton, Dublin, 13.
      (1/7/95)

12   Theresa Doran, Clontarf, Dublin, 3.
      (17/8/96)

13   June Hurley, Killiney, Co Dublin.
      (17/9/88)

14   Mary A Coffey, Kilmacthomas,
      Co Waterford. (29/7/89)

15   Clare O'Brien-Moran, Mackney,
      Ballinasloe, Co Galway. (11/11/95)

16   Contact local Wildlife Ranger

17   Fenella Delap, Shannon, Co Clare.
      (8/92)

18   Andrew Ellis, Roundwood,
      Co Wicklow. (14/9/91)

19   Owen Jacob, Dun Laoghaire,
      Co Dublin. (12/10/91)

20   Nicola Powell, Castletown, Athboy,
      Co Meath. (15/4/89)

21   James Shovlin, Rathbawn Avenue,
      Castlebar, Co Mayo. (20/5/89)

22   Jane Howe, Abbeyleix, Co Laois.
      (20/11/93)

23   Michael Reynolds, Ballydoreen,
      Ashford, Co Wicklow. (9/1/93)

24   Heather Perdue, The Deanery,
      Killaloe, Co Clare. (22/7/89)

25   E W, Cork. (24/11/90)

26   V Denton, Rathfarnham, Dublin.
      (8/12/90)

27   Clive R Symmins, Macetown, Tara,
      Co Meath. (12/5/90)

28   Dany Fauconnier-Swan, Brussels.
      (20/6/92)

29   Virginia Chipperfield, Rathfarnham,
      Dublin, 14. (1/12/89)

30   Geraldine J Gahan, Killinane,
      Dunlavin, Co Kildare. (18/11/89)

Chapter 10
Sprinting with Dolphins

1   Laura, Conlon-McKenna, Kilmacud,
      Dublin, 14. (17/12/88)

2   Viola Barrow, Dublin, Road, Dublin,
      13. (27/10/90)

3   Paddy Doran, Baldoyle, Dublin, 13.
      (5/10/96)

4   Corry O'Reilly, Westport, Co Mayo.
      (25/6/88)

5   Roy Smith, Rowallane Gardens,
      Saintfield, Co Down. (7/7/90)

6   Padraig Greenan, Malahide,
      Co Dublin. (18/8/90)

7   Kevin Swan, Sutton, Dublin. (2/7/88)

8   Tony Beese, Old Blackrock Road,
      Cork. (11/7/92)

9   Marian Clarke, Barna, Co Galway.
      (18/7/92)

10   Reg Roynan, Westport, Co Mayo.
      (7/9/91)

11   Keith Malcolm, Blackrock,
      Co Dublin. (20/6/92)

12   Terry O'Neill, Tralong, Rosscarbery,
      Co Cork. (11/7/92)

13   Louie Ann McDonogh, Quilty,
      Co Clare. (1/4/89)

14   Eleanor Prestage, Limerick. (4/2/95)

15   Clodagh Ruddy, Templeogue, Dublin,
      6W. (5/10/91)

16   Barry Devon, Glenageary, Co Dublin.
      (21/8/93)

17   Gabriel King, Dun Laoghaire,
      Co Dublin. (2/5/92)

Chapter 11
So Bright they would cut your eyes ...

1   John McMahon, Clonsilla, Dublin,
      15. (7/5/88)

2   Clare Harpur, Dalkey, Co Dublin,
      (25/2/89)

3   L Sheeran, Castleknock, Dublin, 15.
      (15/4/89)

4   Ian Rippey, British Butterfly
      Conservation Society, 13 Enniscrone
      Park, Portadown, Co Armagh.
      (27/1/90)

5   John McMahon, Clonsilla, Dublin,
      15. (23/4/94)

6   Nick Harman, Tully Lodge,
      Louisburgh, Co Mayo. (20/5/95).

7   Joseph Kelly, Blackrock, Co Dublin.
      (10/5/97)

8   Cliff and Joyce Christie. (9/12/89)

9   Hugh Massy, Rathkeale, Co Limerick.
      (7/10/95)

10   Rosemary Rudd, Waterville,
      Co Kerry. (14/5/88)

11   Michael Salter, Dundalk, Co Louth.
      (6/6/92)

12 John McMahon, Clonsilla, Dublin, 15. (Eye Extra April 1994)

13 Nick Harman, Tully Lodge, Louisburgh, Co Mayo. (6/7/96)

14 Caroline Bonham, Castlepollard, Co Westmeath. (21/9/96)

15 Eugene Kelly, Glenageary, Co Dublin. (26/4/97)

16 Michael Salter, Dundalk, Co Louth. (6/6/92)

17 Brian Berry, (Eye Extra May 1997)

18 Bob Aldwell, Newtownpark, Blackrock, Co Dublin. (4/7/92)

19 R K Page, Grange Con, Co Wicklow. (12/8/89).

20 Wyn Beere, Orwell Road, Rathgar, Dublin, 6. (26/8/89)

21 Aidan J ffrench, Graduate Parks Supt, Dublin, Corporation. (2/9/89).

22 Padraig Gibbons, Hillcrest Park, Dublin, 11.
David Rowe, Sandyford, Co Dublin. (23/9/89)

23 Patrick Madden, Straffan, Co Kildare, (23/9/89)

24 Kevin Collins, Clonmel, Co Tipperary. (23/9/89)

25 Ian Rippey, Portadown, Co Armagh. (23/9/89)

26 Jack O'Reilly, Clonmel, Co Tipperary. (27/1/96)

27 Milo Kane, Bettyglen, Dublin, 5. (16/9/95)

28 Ian Rippey, Portadown, Co Armagh. (30/11/91)

29 Paddy Lysaght, Thomondgate, Limerick. (9/7/88)

30 Loretta Carney, Kilkenny. (24/8/91)

31 William Kehoe, Killarney, Co Kerry. (24/8/91)

32 Freda Yates, Kilkenny. (17/5/97)

33 Conor Shanley, Castleknock, Co Dublin. (25/6/88)

34 Caitlin and Conor Bent, Tallaght, Co Dublin. (6/10/90)

35 Bernadette Murphy, Loughrea, Co Galway. (9/7/94)

36 Dorothy and Terry Meakin, Kilcoole, Co Wicklow. (6/8/88)

37 Rosemary Rudd, Waterville, Co Kerry (14/5/88); Henry Deegan, Foxford,

Co Mayo (16/9/89); Canon Hardon, Johnstone, Thomastown, Co Kilkenny. (2/11/91); Wyn Beere, Clonskeagh, Dublin, 14 (16/11/91); Ian Rippey, Portadown, Co Armagh (30/11/91); Bob Aldwell, Newtownpark Ave, Blackrock, Co Dublin, (22/9/90; 4/7/92); Jim Leonard, Tramore, Co Waterford. (31/12/93); Jim Fox, Athy, Co Kildare.

38 *Millennium Butterfly Atlas.* Records of Fieldwork from Ireland to: Mary Willis, 18 Charleville Road, Rathmines, Dublin, 6.

Chapter 12
Elephants and Hummingbirds

1 Jim Dawson, South Circular Road, Limerick. (2/11/91)

2 F S Magan, Valentia Island, Co Kerry. (6/10/90)

3 John Draper, Kilpedder, Co Wicklow. (1/7/89)

4 F P Mongey, Tramore, Co Waterford. (27/6/93)

5 Joan Bird, Lusk, Co Dublin. (24/5/97)

6 Siobhán Montgomery, Churchill, Co Donegal. (6/8/94)

7 Joy Simpson, Dun Laoghaire, Co Dublin. (20/7/96)

8 J S Glendinning, Kinsale, Co Cork. (25/5/96)

9 Joan Gallie, Broadford, Co Kildare. (27/10/90)

10 Tom Fewer, Woodstown, Co Waterford. (7/6/97)

11 Peter Toffell, Caherdaniel, Co Kerry. (30/5/92)

12 Ann Durcan, Ballina, Co Mayo. (5/7/97)

13 Eimear Holohan, Clogheen Co Cork. (27/8/88)

14 Conor, Sinclair, Donegal. (16/3/91)

15 Raymond F Haynes (who was the migrant insect recorder for Ireland), 8 "Little Dorking", Mill Road, Killarney, Co Kerry. (7/5/88)

16 Diarmuid Ó Gráda, Roebuck Road, Dublin, 14. (29/1/94)

17 Aoife O'Leary, Clonard, Co Wexford. (2/10/93)

18 Mimi Crowley, Ardmore, Co Waterford. (5/10/91)

19 V Davidson, Enniskillen, Co Fermanagh. (21/9/91)

20 Jim and Howard Fox, Coursetown House, Athy, Co Kildare. (19/11/88)

21 Jim Fox, Coursetown House, Athy, Co Kildare. (4/11/89)

22 Jim Fox, Coursetown House, Athy, Co Kildare. (1/12/90)

23 Mimi Crowley, Carigaline, Co Cork. (20/10/90)

24 Eoin Mooney, Sandymount, Dublin, 4. (9/10/93)

25 R Harrison, Bantry, Co Cork. (13/2/93)

26 Mimi Crowley, Ardmore, Co Waterford. (20/10/90)

27 David Casey, O'Connell Avenue, Limerick. (24/11/90)

28 J S Glendenning, Kinsale, Co Cork. (22/8/92)

29 Tom Quinn, Burriscarra, Claremorris, Co Mayo. (3/8/96)

30 Rosemary Lucas, Killeenmore House, Sallins, Co Kildare. (7/7/90)

31 Theresa Doran, Clontarf, Dublin, 3. (17/8/96)

32 A K Gallie, Broadford, Co Kildare. (30/8/97)

33 Mary Hunt, Kilpedder, Co Wicklow. (12/10/91)

Chapter 13

Myriad Manifold and Multicoloured

1 Bonnie Flanagan, Stillorgan, Co Dublin. (17/9/88)

2 Betty Balcomb, Townparks, Skerries, Co Dublin. (26/8/89)

3 Stephen Butler, Palmerstown, Co Dublin. (27/1/90)

4 Margaret Segrave, Rathfarnham, Dublin, 14. (3/11/90)

5 Harry Kenney, Highfield Park, Galway. (3/9/94)

6 Beatrice Aird-O'Hanlon, Greystones, Co Wicklow. (8/7/95)

7 Brynhild McConnell, Clonkeagh Road, Dublin, 6. (6/8/88)

8 Fergus Kelly, Palmerstown Road, Dublin, 6. (21/9/91)

9 Puzzled, Cashel, Connemara, Co Galway. (19/8/95)

10 Liam and Enda Roche, Castle Road, Saggart, Co Dublin. (23/11/96)

11 Dervilla McKeith, Kilcloon, Co Meath. (20/5/97)

12 James O'Shea, Killarney, Co Kerry. (15/6/97)

13 J Garrett Yates, Naas, Co Kildare. (9/10/93)

14 Catherine Ryan, Castlerea, Co Roscommon. (31/8/96)

15 Geoff Michael, New Ross, Co Wexford. (8/7/95)

16 Ted Dooley, Kanturk, Co Cork. (20/10/90)

17 Harry Bond, Enniscorthy, Co Wexford. (22/10/88)

18 John M O'Connell, Blarney, Co Cork. (15/7/95)

19 Brian and Winnie Murdoch, Rathfarnham, Dublin, 14. (13/8/94)

20 Harry Bond, Killuran, Enniscorthy, Co Wexford. (10/5/97)

21 Carmel Hourigan, Muckross, Killarney, Co Kerry. (26/9/92)

22 Honor Stuart, Goatstown, Dublin, 14. (26/7/97)

23 Heather Russell, Bird Avenue, Clonskeagh, Dublin, 14. (26/7/97)

24 Deirdre Brennan, Dalkey, Co Dublin. (10/9/94)

25 Alison Deegan, North Great George's St, Dublin. (28/8/93)

26 S Heating, Clonduff, Rosenalis, Co Laois. (12/8/89)

27 Michael Leahy, Glencolumbcille, Co Donegal. (16/4/88)

28 Pat Daly, Drumcondra, Dublin, 9. (27/2/93)

29 Susan Flynn, Ballybrack, Co Dublin. (24/8/96)

30 Colm O'Regan, Dripaey, Co Cork. (7/9/91)

31 Henry Deegan, Rathfarnham, Dublin, 14. (29/8/92)

32 Diana Gishing, Kinsale, Co Cork. (2/6/90)

33 John Gardner, Beechgrove Gardens, Belfast. (7/11/92)

34 Tony Cullen, Kimmage Road, Dublin, 6. (2/8/97)

35 Eamon Grennan, Renvyle, Co Galway. (30/7/97)

36 Mary Ryan, Nenagh, Co Tipperary. (30/3/96)

37 Gillies Macbain, Cranagh Castle, Co Tipperary. (25/6/88; 2/8/97)

38 Joseph Clancy, Booterstown, Co Dublin.

39 Larry Kenny, Ferns, Co Wexford. (25/8/90)

40 Eric F Mayne, Bangor, Co Down. (1/4/89)

41 Fred Walker, Wicklow. (9/2/91)

42 F X Burke, Northbrook Road, Dublin, (27/8/88)

43 H Melville, Dartry, Dublin, 6. (12/8/89)

44 Nial O'Kennedy, Blackrock, Co Dublin. (22/10/94)

45 Christine Keaney, Claregalway, Co Galway. (15/7/95)

46 Kevin Flanagan, Limerick. (12/2/94)

47 Robert Gallagher, Manorhamilton, Co Leitrim. (28/12/91)

48 N Cahalan, Loch Dubh, Tahilla, Co Kerry (9/7/88; 20/8/88)

49 Barbara Deegan, Rathfarnham, Dublin, 14. (20/2/93)

50 Betty White, Ashford, Co Wicklow. (27/3/93)

51 T Lockhart, Rathfarnham, Dublin, 16. (16/10/93)

52 Michael Fewer, Ballyboden, Dublin, 16. (17/12/88)

53 Kevin Kiely, Gortlee, Letterkenny, Co Donegal. (23/3/96)

54 Michael Fewer, Glendoher Road, Dublin, 16. (10/6/95)

Chapter 14
Orgies in the Pond

1 Norma Malcolm, Carrignagaw, Lismore, Co Waterford. (25/2/89)

2 David Leach, Woodford, Co Galway. (10/3/90)

3 Ursula O'Leary, Dun Laoghaire, Co Dublin. (7/4/90)

4 S Pruzina, Newry, Co Down. (6/3/93)

5 Imogen Stuart, Sandycove, Co Dublin. (1/3/97)

6 J W Parker, Blackrock, Co Dublin. (22/12/90)

7 Patrick Madden, Straffan, Co Kildare. (29/2/92)

8 N P Delaney, Dun Laoghaire, Co Dublin. (16/8/97)

9 Claire Walsh and Professor Frank Mitchell, TCD. (12/11/94)

10 Ursula O'Leary, Dun Laoghaire, Co Dublin. (7/4/90)

11 Judik Hutchinson, Blackrock, Co Dublin. (10/9/88)

12 See *A Year's Turning* by Michael Viney, Blackstaff Press, 1996.

13 Brian Mayne, Killiney, Co Dublin. (30/7/88)

14 Denis Hamill, Santry, Dublin. (7/12/91)

15 Aideen Cresswell, Kilternan, Co Dublin. (16/10/93)

16 Jim Delaney, Hodson Bay, Co Westmeath. (27/6/92)

17 Nick Becker, Rathdrum, Co Wicklow. (18/12/93)

18 Margaret Thompson, Shankill, Co Dublin. (28/9/96)

19 F J Fitzsimons, Drumbracken, Carrickmacross, Co Monaghan. (18/6/94)

20 Deirdre Toohey, Oranmore, Co Galway. (25/5/91)

21 June Hurley, Killiney, Co Dublin. (17/9/88)

22 Gillies Macbain, Cranagh Castle, Templemore, Co Tipperary. (3/8/91)

23 Patricia Fogarty, Palmerstown, Dublin, 20. (13/8/94)

24 M T Archdale, Omagh, Co Tyrone. (4/4/92)

25 Edward Horan, Sligo. (5/7/97).

26 Richard Ennis, Castlemaine, Co Kerry. (6/8/94)

27 Nancy O'Flynn, Blackrock, Co Dublin. (4/5/97)

Chapter 15

Strangers on the Shore

1 Robbie Fitzpatrick, Aughfad, Taghmon, Co Wexford. (24/2/90)

2 Joe Little, Blackrock, Co Dublin. (12/10/91)

3 Doris Murdoch, Killiney, Co Dublin. (16/2/91)

4 Sarah Laird, Kilbride, Co Wicklow. (17/2/96)

5 Marilyn Hearn, Tramore, Co Waterford. (6/4/91)

6 Paul V Horsman in *Marine Life*, Croom Helm, 1985.

7 Louie Ann McDonagh, Quilty, Co Clare. (28/3/92)

8 Eugene Doran, Dun Laoghaire, Co Dublin. (21/8/93)

9 Anthony Carroll, Clifden, Co Galway. (11/9/93)

10 Ethne Miles, Churchtown, Dublin, 14. (18/9/93)

11 Roger Grimes, Rossmindle, Westport, Co Mayo. (29/7/95)

12 G M Patton, Kilberry, Navan, Co Meath. (13/11/93)

13 Jim Hurley, Grange, Kilmore, Co Wexford. (18/11/95)

14 Mildred Weekes, Lismore, Co Waterford. (2/12/95)

15 Stephen O'Connor, Castletroy, Co Limerick. (15/4/89)

16 George Ball, Clontarf, Dublin, 3.(2/10/93)

17 Dixie Collins, Kilkee, Co Clare. (20/2/93)

18 Ellen-Nesta Dick, Skreen, Co Sligo. (9/2/91)

19 Evelyn Musgrave, Cleggan, Co Galway. (2/2/91)

20 Barbara Allen, Stranmillis, Belfast. (9/11/91).

21 Philip Smyly, (Director), Strand Road, Dublin, 4. (1/7/97)

22 David Gilligan, Naas Sub-Aqua Club, Co Kildare. (20/1/90)

23 A Mulcahy,Meelick, Co Clare. (5/10/91)

24 "Trigger fish species in Irish Waters", by D T Quigley, K Flannery and J

O'Shea, Biogeography of Ireland: *Past, Present and Future*, ed. M J Costello & K S Kelly; Irish Biogeographical Society, 1993.

25 Patrick Palmer, Beaumont, Dublin, 9. (22/6/96)

Chapter 16

Long Live the Weeds

1 Jack R Whaley, Kells, Co Meath. (23/4/88)

2 Brigid O'Donnell, Redford, Culdaff, Co Donegal. (30/9/89)

3 Máire Nic Mhaoláin, Deilginis, Co Atha Chliath. (28/10/89)

4 Eileen Kilroy, Gort, Co Galway. (30/4/88)

5 Carmel Hourigan, Muckross, Killarney, Co Kerry. (21/5/88)

6 M J O'Connor, Quilty, Co Clare. (12/1/91)

7 Colm Faughnan, Letterkenny, Co Donegal. (17/2/96)

8 Teresa McGowan. Kinlough, Co Leitrim. (25/5/96)

9 Carol Stephenson, Monkstown, Co Dublin. (25/11/89)

10 Rosamund Lombard, Portroe, Nenagh, Co Tipperary. (4/3/89)

11 D Clifford, Ballymakegogue, Fenit, Co Limerick. (2/7/88)

12 Yvonne Power, Kilminnin, Dungarvan, Co Waterford. (24/6/89)

13 Paul Carroll, Pike of Rushall, Portlaoise. (4/6/94)

14 Geoffrey Dean, Ballsbridge, Dublin, 4. (14/5/94)

15 Larry Power, Mount Merrion, Co Dublin. (21/5/88)

16 Jim Davies, Merthyr Tydfil, Mid-Glamorgan. (15/12/90)

17 Dermot Edwards, Lismore, Co Waterford. (12/6/93)

18 Peter Brown, Dundrum, Dublin, 16. (14/3/92)

19 P Ryan, Ennis Road, Limerick. (9/7/88)

20 Patrick Madden, Straffan, Co Kildare. (13/5/89)

21 *Go wild at School* by Patrick Madden, School Wildlife Garden Association 1996; £4.95

22 Sandro Cafolla, Design by Nature, Monivea Cross, Crettyard, Co Carlow.

23 Brigid Flanagan, Dundalk, Co Louth. (22/10/94)

24 Rosamund Sterling, Coolbawn, Nenagh, Co Tipperary. (9/11/96)

25 Rosemary Goodbody, Athenry, Co Galway.

26 Mary Harney, Ennis, Co Clare.

27 Ronan Henderson, Roundstone, Co Galway. (3/9/88)

28 John Maynard, Croghan, Boyle, Co Roscommon. (26/9/92)

29 Brigid O'Donnell, Redford, Culdaff, Co Donegal. (30/9/89)

30 Joan Hartness, Corbally, Limerick. (16/9/89)

31 F J Fitzsimons, Carrickmacross, Co Monaghan. (22/10/94)

32 Denis Byrne, Blackrock, Co Dublin. (23/8/97)

33 Robert Hayes, Farnham Road, Cavan. (4/3/89)

34 Eimer Morris, Drumree, Co Meath. (2/11/91)

35 Paul Kennedy, Harold's Cross, Dublin, 6W. (19/3/94)

36 Gay Hackett, Raheny, Dublin, 5 (20/1/96)

37 Michael Cleary, Ballyhaunis, Co Mayo. (16/11/91)

38 Brian Ó Crávshey, Culdaff, Lifford, Co Donegal. (11/11/89)

39 Peter Dempster, Conna, Co Cork. (3/6/95)

40 Alan McClintock, Coolbawn, Nenagh, Co Tipperary. (21/7/90)

41 Gerry Bracken, Harbour House, Westport, Co Mayo. (17/12/88)

42 Irene Deisler, Crucknagerragh, Dungloe, Co Donegal. (14/5/88)

43 M Fagan, Sweetmount Avenue, Dublin, 14. (1/4/89)

44 *For Love of Trees* by Risteard Mulcahy, Environmental Publications, 1996.

45 M O Fogarty, Aughrim, Co Wicklow. (2/12/89)

46 Jack O'Reilly, Clonmel, Co Tipperary. (29/5/93)

47 Pamela McCourt Francescone, Via del Magliana, Rome. (20/10/90)

48 Kenneth Mills, Ballyboden, Dublin, 16. (11/5/91)

49 Mark Glynn, Tallaght, Dublin, 24. (9/12/95)

50 Bob Curran, Dalkey, Co Dublin. (10/8/91)

Chapter 17
Over the Rainbow

1 Lorraine and Howard Marshall, Kildorrery, Co Cork. (8/2/97)

2 Tim Robinson, Roundstone, Co Galway. (16/2/91)

3 G Bennett, Bishopstown, Co Cork. (18/1/92)

4 Sara Cleary, Dunmore East, Co Waterford. (11/12/93)

5 Margaret Casey, Churchtown, Dublin, 14.

6 Gerry McNamara, Loughinisland, Downpatrick, Co Down. (9/12/89)

USEFUL ADDRESSES

Birdwatch Ireland
(with local branches)
(formerly Irish Wildbird
Conservancy)
Ruttledge House, Dublin, 2.
8 Longford Place, Monkstown
Co Dublin.
Tel: 01 2804322;
Fax: 01 2844407
e-mail: bird@indigo.ie

The Irish Whale and Dolphin
Group
c/o Dept of Zoology (local co-
ordinators)
University College Cork
Tel: 021 904053;
Fax: 021 277922

The Royal Society for the
Protection of Birds
(RSPB - Local branches in NI)
Belvoir Park Forest
Belfast BT 8 4QT
Tel: 01232 491547;
Fax: 0121 491669

Conservation Volunteers Ireland
The Green, Griffith College
South Circular Road, Dublin, 8
Tel: 01 4547185

Irish Wildlife Trust
(local branches)
107 Lower Baggot Street
Dublin, 2.
Tel: 01 676 8588;
Fax: 01 676 8601
e-mail: enquiries@iwt.ie

Record of Fieldwork from Ireland
for *Millennium Butterfly Atlas* to:

Trevor Boyd
12 Woodland Avenue
Helen's Bay
Bangor, Co Down
Tel: 01247 852276
e-mail: boydtd@aol.com

or

Mary Willis,
18 Charleville Road
Rathmines, Dublin, 6.

Ulster Wildlife Trust
3 New Line
Crossgar, Co Down
Tel: 01 396 830282

Irish Peatlands Conservation
Council
119 Capel Street, Dublin, 1
Tel/Fax: 01 8722397
e-mail: ipcc@indigo.ie
Web site:
http//aoife.indigo.ie/~ipcc

INDEX

MAMMAL TRACKS

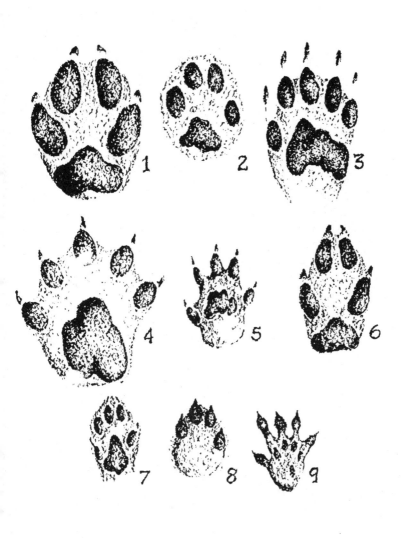

1. Dog	2. Cat	3. Badger
4. Otter	5. Mink	6. Fox
7. Stoat	8. Rabbit	9. Hedgehog

Can you tell me what it might be?

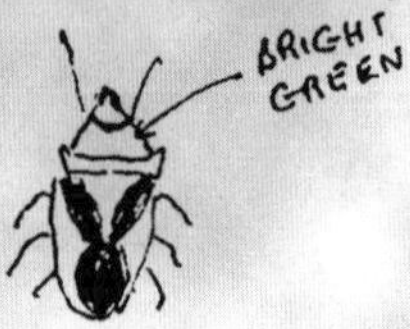

BRIGHT GREEN

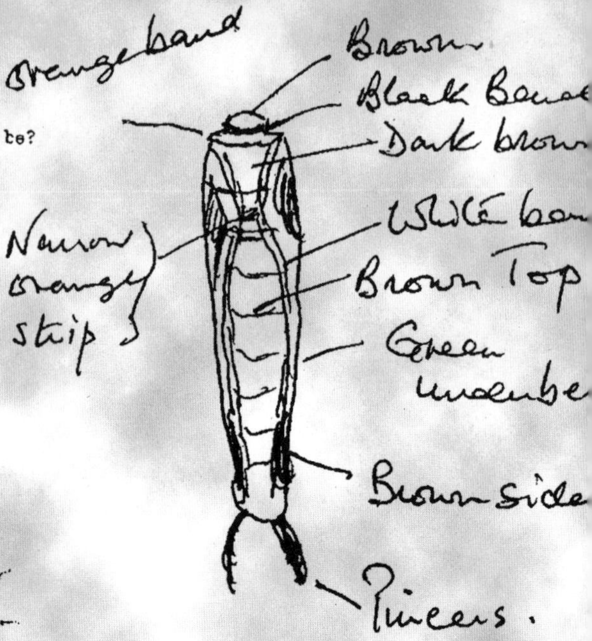

Orange band

Brown
Black Bead
Dark brown

White band

Brown Top

Green underbe[...]

Brown side

Pincers.

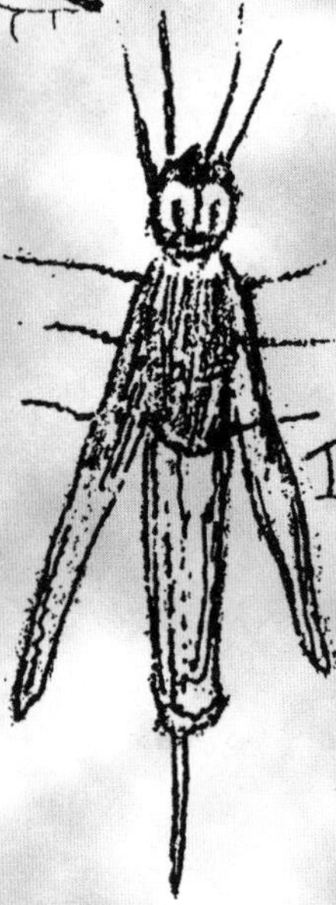

Narrow orange strip

It was something like this ---

many antennae looked very fierce

mussel-like sh[...]
+ colouring, but from jelly-like.

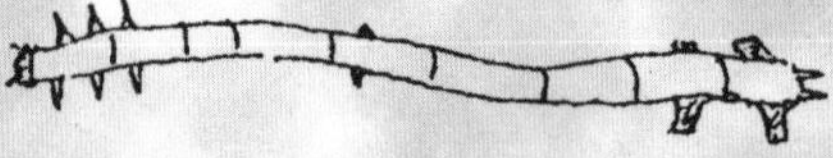

WHEN YOU POKE HIM HE DOES
SIDE VIEW THIS. WHAT DOES HE

GROW INTO?

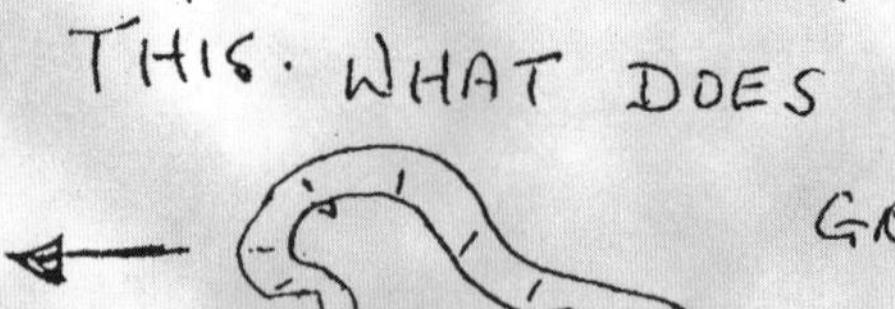